Unbecoming

Mingyan (Iris) Liu

First Edition Design Publishing
Sarasota, Florida USA

Unbecoming
Copyright ©2022 Mingyan (Iris) Liu

ISBN 978-1-506-910-62-8 PBK
ISBN 978-1-506-910-63-5 EBK

August 2022

Published and Distributed by
First Edition Design Publishing, Inc.
P.O. Box 17646, Sarasota, FL 34276-3217
www.firsteditiondesignpublishing.com

ALL RIGHTS RESERVED. No part of this book publication may be reproduced, stored in a retrieval system, or transmitted in any form or by any means — electronic, mechanical, photocopy, recording, or any other — except brief quotation in reviews, without the prior permission of the author or publisher.

From the Author

Dear Reader:

My name is Iris Liu. I am a Graduating Senior from Manhasset High School.

I've always struggled with being good enough. Good enough grades. Good enough social skills. Good enough time management skills. Good enough writing. The list goes on and on.

Whenever I failed to meet the expecta-tions others or the expectations that I set for myself, I would just stop doing everything. What's the point if it's not good enough? It was especially devastating when I would try everything to meet those expectations but still fail - because it was a final verdict that I am simply not good enough. No matter what I did, I was just *unbecoming*. Unbecoming to my family, *unbecoming* to the Iris others thought of me as, and *unbecoming* to the Iris I wanted to become.

But the truth is I was and always will be *unbecoming*, in one way or another.

The Asian American community as a whole is "Unbecoming." Because of the model minority stereo-type, we are portrayed as quiet, meek, and unfit for leadership. Our accent is *unbecoming*. Our culture is *unbecoming*. Our food is *unbecoming*.

So I dedicate this book to being UNBECOMING. I do not meet the standards others and I have set for myself. But in challenging and reflecting on my *unbecomingness* in both society's and my own eyes, I've discovered new depths to who I view myself as. As I challenge my *unbecomingness* as a quiet girl, I've learned to speak up for myself and others.

In reflecting on how others view my *unbecomingness*, I've gained new insights.

Therefore, even though "Unbecoming" has a negative connotation, it also means growth and progress - which is what this book reflects.

This book is a collection of my writing exploring my identity from sixth to eleventh grade. I hope you enjoy it. And for all the writers and students who don't think you are good enough, maybe you aren't. We just have to deal with that. But who cares? Try your best, enjoy yourself, and at the end of the day, if you still come out *unbecoming*, at least you know there was no other way the story could have ended.

Best wishes,
The Unbecoming Mingyan (Iris) Liu

Contents

Chapter 1
When I Just Started Writing 1
Immigration Experiences to America 1

Chapter 2
Everyone Has To Start From Somewhere 5
A Ghost Story 5
Lazy Susan 16
My Perfect Plan to Become the President of the United
States 20
Open Letter to the Chinese Community 24

Chapter 3
Experimentation & Reflection Leads to Progress 27
Dream Baker 27
Family Dinner 48
The Obstacle Course 54
An Open Letter to the Educational Department of New
York State 57

Chapter 4
Challenging Myself 76
Potstickers 76
The Quiet Girl 80
We Are Not Victims - Why the Asian and Black
Community needs Coalition 82
What Does Being An Immigrant Mean? 85

Chapter I

When I Just Started Writing

(Sixth Grade)

Immigration Experiences to America

This memoir was written in sixth grade as a school assignment and then was submitted to The Nassau County Reading Council Contest for Young Authors by my English Teacher. This was my first essay on my identity. It's full of grammar mistakes and awkward sentences. The sixth-grade Iris still didn't quite understand the English Language yet.

Life is always full of change, nothing ever remains the same. I had a perfect life, I had great friends, good grades, and I was really happy with my life in China. Everything was just the way it should be.

When I was eight. My parents took me on a trip to America. We were looking for a house, a house we could live in when we moved here two years later. America was beautiful. The shadow of the green trees covered the lush yard. The smell of fresh cut grass was floating in the clean air and people were smiling to each other as they walked on the street. We had chosen a beautiful red brick house with red roses dancing in the air like fire pink roses showing off their beauty and then dandelions flying by if they had wings. My mind kept wandering off, wondering what life would be like when we moved to America. But I couldn't find an answer. I just hope that everything would be fine.

One sunny day during this vacation, my brother and I were playing in our hotel room, jumping up and down on the bed and singing funny songs. Laughter was everywhere. The calm and joyful wood were suddenly interrupted by a huge noise made by the door as my mom quickly ran into the room and said "We are moving to America. Now." The world seemed to come out in slow motion and the room started spinning fast.

I screamed. "WHAT! NO! HOW! WHY!"

My brother wasn't taking the news too well either. He stared into the space, horrified, as if he had seen an alien.

Then my my mom said. "I know this is way too sudden for you guys, but I just figured the earlier we come here, the easier it will be for you guys to fit in."

I fell on the bed, opened my mouth and said quietly. "I just need a second to recover, just a second..." My head was full of buzzing noise and I thought *This crazy! No way! We're coming to live here now?* But after a while I recovered and thought maybe it would be fine. So I sat up and said "Alright, let's get packing."

When we first came to America, it was very harsh. We couldn't understand most of the things people said and we had to get used to a new home, a new country, a new school and new friends. My whole life seemed to turn upside down. I was lonely at school because I didn't know how to speak English too well, so I had no courage to talk to people. The sky always looked grey and sad. I couldn't understand my homework or classwork and sometimes I knew what I wanted to say but didn't know how. At recess I sat with a group of girls, but I was just watching and listening. Sometimes I would smile a little, but most of the time you would only see me with my book, wondering and reading.

I always hoped and dreamed that maybe, just maybe, things would get better. That a girl my age from China would come and we would be friends. I hoped and wish to go back to China, to my old happy life. But deep down inside me I knew if I could be brave and talk to others, I would make great friends and everything would be fine. But I just couldn't do it.

One day a girl came along. She had long, curly black hair, big watery eyes at a round cheek with a sweet smile on it. Her name was Kelly. That day was the day everything changes. I am wearing my lucky pink Tutu. That afternoon my ELA teacher told me "Iris, I have a mission to give you."

I replied. "What is it?"

"Do you know the New Girl, Kelly?"

"Yeah."

"I want you to invite her to play with you at recess."

"Ummm...ok!" So I did. I invited her to play with me and we ended up playing with other girls too. We all played tag, running like crazy, laughing till recess was over. Sky seemed to brighten up a little, but just a little.

From that day on, everything came back to me. I played with Kelly every day. Everyone in the school knew we were best friends. We always knew what the other was thinking and we always talked and played with each other. I'm also good at school now, my grades speed up lightning fast and now I can get 100 on tests almost every time. Now I smile at the girl with the pink tutu in the mirror. This is the girl I know, the girl with friends, with good grades and who is always smiling. I know this girl has landed on the bright side, the pink tutus is the girl's parachute. And the sky seemed so blue and clear.

Chapter 2

Everyone Has To Start From Somewhere

(Ninth Grade)

A Ghost Story

Fiction. Published by local school magazine - Phoenix. Won best writing in Karie Sit Contest, honorable mention in the Phyliss J. Mccarthy scholarship, and Scholastics Gold Key.

On the day I met the boy, the ghosts and I were singing the Chinese folk song, 茉莉花, or *Jasmine Flower*. Some of us sounded like the blowing of a gentle breeze in the autumn night; some of us sounded like a bell, and I sounded like the soft crackles of a fireplace. The harmonious melody of our voices turned into rats being choked to death when we noticed a boy standing at the gate of the graveyard. At first glance, I thought he was another one of us because of how thin and scrawny he was. But the determination and spark in his eyes couldn't have belonged to any ghost.

"What is he doing here?" Yuxin, the blacksmith exclaimed. "He's going to scare away our audience!"

"Could he be lost?" MeiWei, the baker asked "Where are his parents? He looks like he's going to fall over."

Visits from humans were rare, and we argued about this strange new visitor. But the boy just stood there, with his mouth agape in wonder and staring so intently at us that I thought that he could... see us? I voiced my concern to the others, but they brushed it off. That's impossible, they said. The boy is lost and will probably go back to his house soon. But my curiosity was too strong to ignore, so when the boy slowly slipped out of the graveyard, I trailed behind.

I could vaguely remember that I grew up in this place, but I didn't recognize it at all. New kinds of metal machines sped past us on the road instead of carriages; houses filled every bit of open land and stood next to each other in rows, and people poked at the thin, black bricks they carried around in their palms.

I watched the boy meander down the stone path to the town and made his way to a small wooden house that looked more like a glorified garden shed. As I slithered into the house, the scent of the living immediately closed in on me. I tried to ignore the urge to zip back to the cemetery as the scent grew stronger. I felt like I was stuffed in three layers of coats on a hot summer day.

"Hey!" A woman exclaimed from the tattered sofa, and she hung up her phone. "How was your day?"

The boy held his hands up and gestured something. His face lit up with a small smile.

"That's great to hear." The woman replied. Exhaustion spread over her like molasses, dragging her eyes and her arms down. But she fought with all her strength to smile at the boy and then handed him a cup with dark liquid.

"Dinner will be ready in one hour. Take your medicine and take a nap, okay?"

The boy gave her a thumbs up and then hugged her. He hopped away from the kitchen and through a small door. In the room, the boy began to dig around in a giant cardboard box. Meanwhile, I floated around, taking the room in. It was clean and organized; a few toys and books were scattered over the desk. The bed had some soft pillows on it but nothing else.

He finally pulled a ragged notebook out from the other junk; perhaps he wanted to do his homework. I thought back to my living days and wondered if I did homework. But my memories were hazy, like corroded old photographs. There was one image I remembered: a boy -- my son -- crying in the closet of his room while I stood outside of his locked doors, saying something about being too busy and that I had to work so our family could be fed.

I figured I had a family, but no one in the town ever made an altar for me on Qing Ming Jie, the day of the dead; it was a special day when everyone would honor their passed family members by presenting their favorite food at their altars. It always made me a little sad when the other ghosts could enjoy a feast with their family on this holiday while I had to stay at the graveyard.

With a flourish, the boy wrote something in his notebook and turned it over. On a piece of loose-leaf paper, he wrote *I can see you.*

"What?" I whispered. I'd never heard of a human that could communicate with a ghost without using some special device. Why was this happening?

The boy's shoulders shook with silent laughter when he saw the shock on my face. He flipped to another page and wrote, *You have a nice voice.*

"I know!" I grinned with triumph. "Not to brag, I have the best voice in the chorus. But uh...how is this possible? Are you some sort of spirit medium?"

The boy shook his head and shrugged. He scribbled, *And how do ghosts work? I thought you guys only existed in fairy tales.*

"Well, you see, child." I tapped him on his head. "Most spirits go to 地府 (*underworld*) when they die to get reincarnated, but those who have an especially strong desire or wish that remained unfulfilled on earth must remain here and attempt, against all odds, to fulfill it. It's really not all that great." I glanced over his head, and he started to write his response. "How come you are writing everything down?"

He hovered over his paper for some time, thinking and staring at a black spider crawling his bed, before finally jotting down the words, *My lungs are not working because I'm sick. It's hard to speak.*

"Ah..." I sat down by him on the bed. "I see, sorry." It must be hard to live without being able to speak,

It's ok. It's not your fault! Maybe we can be ghost friends in the future

"But you have to have a really strong unfulfilled desire to become a ghost," I pondered. "What do you still have to do here on Earth?"

The boy pointed at the roof above us. Ugly rusted pipes dangled stiffly; water dripped down through the cracks. I grew anxious watching the boy stand under it.

I want to fix our roof. The boy frowned. *My parents spent all of our money on my treatment. I overheard that it would take a total of 45,000 yuan in order to fix it.*

Talking with this boy was the first real interaction I've had since I died. Don't get me wrong, and the other ghosts are nice too. It's just that no one else died in the same time period as me, so there was little we could talk about aside from our song rehearsals. During the 18 years that I spent as a ghost, I'd grown numb to life. But I missed the smell of a rainy day, the scratch of a phonograph record, and the taste of steamed buns. I wished to live again. Although that was impossible to achieve, at least I could still help the boy. Being forced to spend the rest of eternity haunting the hollow caverns of your grave is an awful fate.

"You know what, I'll make sure you fulfill your wish and get to reincarnate. Pinkie promise."

The boy's eyes shone with excitement, and he scrambled to write, *Thank you!!*

"Alright, let's brainstorm. Do you have any ideas?"

The boy clicked the pen repeatedly, then wrote, *we can start a lemonade shop.*

Of course, a kid would think that. I chuckled. "A lemonade stand is a nice thought, but it would take years before we could even get enough money for half of the roof."

The boy nodded. *What about a car wash?*

"I don't think your body can handle that much work."

You're right.

He was unfazed by these first few misses, and so we kept scribbling down ideas: cleaning other people's houses, tutoring students, and selling handmade jewelry. These were all nice thoughts, but none seemed likely to work.

The boy gave a frustrated huff and gestured to the outside. He seemed a bit down, so I figured that getting a breath of fresh air would lift his spirit.

As we wandered into a plaza, the sense of the living got more and more suffocating. The boy wheezed from exertion, so I told him to rest on the bench. When I looked around, there were vendors selling hot dogs and fried rice, people chatting and laughing, and musicians playing well-polished instruments.

Musicians? Musicians!

That word lit up my world like a brilliant firework. Why hadn't I thought of it earlier!? All my worries were lifted from my body, and I knew exactly what to do. I hovered over the boy and linked a part of my soul to him.

Suddenly, I could feel the wind blowing against my face, and the sunshine touched my skin instead of passing right through it. It had been so long since I tasted fresh air, and I gulped down as many breaths as I could. But it was difficult to appreciate being alive again when I felt like my lungs were being compressed by all the living presence next to me.

Okay, you can do this, I said to myself and placed the boy's hat in front of him. You've performed in front of audiences much larger than this one. Just breathe.

I closed my eyes and started to sing. When people turned to look, they saw a boy in torn jeans singing in a voice that sounded like a dying fire; the partial link between our souls only allowed a narrow strand of my voice to travel through him. The air grew increasingly heavy, and my voice wobbled when the slightest wind blew. This is as far as partial possession could get us. Yet a complete link between our souls would endanger the boy's health, and that is the last thing I wanted. Still determined, I clenched my fist and sang through the feeling of suffocation.

And it happened. People started tossing change into the hat. At first, it wasn't much, but soon there was more and more. We were a sensation.

Later, back in the boy's room, he rested. *That was amazing*! He gestured at his notepad wildly. He rolled around in his bed while I sat on the window sill. I smiled. It was wonderful to have an appreciating audience, especially when my singing was also helping him get what he needed.

"Let's see how much you've got."

The kid scattered the money and coins onto the floor. I helped him organize the spare change and found out we had made almost 200 yuan. It was a small dent in our goal, but it seemed to cheer up the boy; he danced around the room while I laughed. Glancing at the sunlight outside the window, I remembered a moment when my son was joyous like this too. I could see him now in my mind's eye running through our living room, holding a toy train over his head, and screaming the way only little children can.

We were excited by our success, but we both knew it would take a lot more work to reach our goal. We traveled back and forth between the town and the house every day. I spent many evenings learning new songs and often worried about the boy's health. I tried to take care of him as best as I could by reminding him to keep warm and to eat. We watched the green leaves turn into brilliant shades of yellow and red. We trampled around in the snow and fed the birds that came back to their nests in spring. I learned that his favorite animal was the giraffe because of its long neck. I even managed to learn some sign language!

When the seasons shifted back to summer, We had raised a little more than 40,000 yuan! The boy was still as bright and optimistic as he was when I first met him, but he was also thin and worn looking.

"You look really tired," I asked one night. "Are you all right?" The boy sat on the bench at the plaza. He smiled weakly and nodded before resting his head gently against the back of the bench, falling into sleep. And it was that moment when I realized what I was doing. I felt a twinge of guilt. I'm wearing his body down; I'm killing him. Why hadn't he said something about this?

The boy woke up minutes later.

"Listen-" I began. "Maybe there is another way we can finish raising money for the roof. We only need another 5,000 yuan. You aren't looking well."

The boy frowned and opened his mouth as if he could speak, but his eyes rolled to the back of his head, and he fell onto the ground.

"Somebody help!" I screamed in horror. People swarmed around us, and a lady picked up the boy. A child screamed. Finally, a man called for help. There were noises and people rushing here and there. I could only watch as the boy was finally hoisted into an ambulance and driven away. Another memory of my past life flashed before my eyes: my son's funeral. It was a gray day. The trees were barren. The air was cold and stung my cheeks. I felt like it was me going into the grave instead of my boy. Every breath felt hollow. A careless driver was all it took to end both of our lives.

At the hospital, the boy had changed into a patient's gown, and he had tubes running into his nose to help him breathe. I paced around the room aimlessly, trying to find something to distract me. I attempted to look at the birds outside the window, but all that I could think about was that another son was going to be taken away from me.

After some time, the boy slowly opened his eyes. "Thank god you're okay," I exclaimed, and the boy signed hello back.

"This was my fault. I don't know what I was thinking, putting you at risk like that."

He found his notepad, and his hand shook as he wrote. *It's okay. I am going to die soon.*

The boy's words chilled me.

The doctor said... he paused to think before writing, *that I have one more week.*

"You should focus on getting better. You should spend the next week with your parents and do the things you love. We'll stop the performances for now."

The boy shook his head violently. *We still don't have enough money.*

"I know, but you should enjoy your last moments with your family."

I can't die peacefully without knowing my family can be happy. I will never forgive myself! I don't want to be a ghost. Please.

We stared at each other in silence. The boy had a point, and, after all, I was the one who had turned his back on his family all those years ago. At least the boy had the courage to bring joy to his one last time.

"Fine." I sighed. "What do you need me to do?"

A full possession. His eyes were filled with determination. *Our last concert in this hospital, one final time.*

I walked over to him, taking a deep breath, before connecting our souls once more. This time, the pain was much greater. I let out a murmur, surprised to hear that our voice was now stable, ready for the performance of a lifetime. I placed the boy's hat onto the floor. His soul was jittering with nerves and excitement.

The clear sound of our voice rang through the entire hospital. It punctured the walls. I decided to sing 茉莉花 (*Jasmine flower*) for our first song, in memory of our first meeting.

One by one, people stopped in our doorway to look. The boy's parents gasped at the sight as tears filled their eyes. I could feel the boy's soul laughing and dancing. I sang all the songs I had learned in the past year, bringing more and more spectators. An old lady cried, and another boy stood there in shock. Reporters quietly came by the doorway and recorded us.

These reporters put us on something called the internet, where we quickly became a star. People joined our singing in their own homes, talking about their sorrows and their stories. They joined together to raise money for the boy's treatment and his illness.

Yet the boy's soul got weaker and weaker. When the fourth day came, I was ejected from his soul, a soul that was no longer glowing with joy or dancing. I looked back at the bed. The boy's breathing slowed, and his eyes dropped.

"Sleep well, buddy," I silently whispered, trying to brush the hair from his eyes. Sorrow gripped me tightly as I slowly drifted out of the room. The hat was filled with money, yet I didn't feel the same joy that I'd felt at our previous performances.

When I got out of the hospital, there was no boy to follow me. Once again, it was just me. Trapped forever.

But then, darkness surrounded me except for a soft light glowing in front of me, radiating warmth. The boy stood inside the light, waving goodbye, and wrapped his arms around my transparent figure in an attempt to hug me. I looked up at him, puzzled.

What was happening? The boy smiled and pointed behind my back. There stood my son, staring at me in disbelief. He wore the brand new red shirt I had bought him the day he'd died. His hair was sticking out in every direction.

    I kneeled down and took him into my arms as the warmth slowly dragged me into an eternal sleep.

Lazy Susan

Personal Memoir

 As a young child, I didn't have any concept of time, but I knew the arrival of the brittle and sharp air and a gray blanket covering the sun meant New Year celebrations would be commencing soon. The chatter in my school would start to spill into the streets and markets, along with the crisp rhythm of firecrackers. Dark buildings at night would be decorated by a sea of bright red and gold lights, along with bright signs advertising "50% off! It's a steal!" And although I didn't like shopping marathons, I was thrilled by the cheerful mood evoked by these corny ads.

 The night of our last family dinner, my mother and I happily pulled on new coral and red dresses with intricate designs of clouds, lotuses, and cranes and bedazzled our hair with glittering hair clips.

 "Can we please go now?" I tried to suppress my bursting excitement and glanced back at my mother. It felt as if we had been in front of the mirror forever! I simply couldn't wait another second.

 "Stay still," my mother scolded as she finally managed to tie my hair up with the small red ribbon she had been holding between her teeth.

 I immediately hopped from the stool and dashed for the door. Bursting with anticipation, all I could think about was the buttery smell of my grandmother's fried mushrooms.

 Arriving at my aunt's cozy apartment, we were greeted by the warm scent of clean laundry and yeast. It was a familiar smell that put my heart at ease, though by now, it had almost fainted from my memory. My aunt stopped for a brief hug before hurrying past me, her arms overflowing with an assortment of beer bottles and glasses. I knew later there would be an elaborate discussion among the dads and uncles of the beer's origins. This was one of the many mysteries I observed at family gatherings; the bottles all looked the same to me.

My aunt's home was eccentric, noisy, and cluttered with bizarre objects that seemed to have no purpose. I found a display of life-like ceramic cats sitting in a variety of poses on the living room shelf to be the most peculiar. I was particularly cautious of the one whose head hung over the edge to stare at guests passing by. It had always seemed that the cat was bound to fall on someone's head, but despite bringing this to my aunt's attention, she and the other adults didn't seem concerned. Just in case, I made sure to cover my head and run when it was necessary to pass this hazard. Looking back, it's funny how much stress and terror a cute ceramic cat brought me. I often think about whether they're still there.

In addition to my private traditions, there were ceremonial events. Each year, the strongest people in my family, usually the dads, would go down to the basement and return with the round wooden table top that was reserved for celebrations. The tabletop was placed on top of the rectangle-shaped dining table, transforming and hiding the original base. It was like the ribbon cutting at our dinners, a formal start to a night of laughter and joy.

My brother and I gathered around the table, tip-toeing to get a peek at the adults finishing the final preparation. Next to each delicately painted plate lay a set of wooden chopsticks, used to protect the sacred dishes reserved for this occasion. The table was modest, and I found comfort in its simplicity.

I traced the scars with my finger while recalling their stories. The trail of dots on the left side was from a dinosaur excavation kit. My brother was careless and had let the tool hit the table too hard, but the Triceratops inside was worth the scolding from our parents, and we soon forgot about the ordeal. Looking back, I see now that my brother and I must've been a handful for my mother. We were always climbing on everything, and our curiosity often got us into trouble. But now we're a lot more mature and definitely wouldn't dream of ruining a table for a triceratops anytime soon.

After exchanging stories and laughs with our relatives, the strongest people in my family, usually the dads, would go down to the basement and return with a rotate-able large glass plate, the crowning jewel of our new year dinner preparation. This rotating platter would serve the role of our non-sentient waiter during dinner, spinning around to deliver food from one person to another. On one side, my grandpa excitedly chatted with my brother about stories of his childhood. On the other side, my aunt poured tea for my grandmother. I sat in the middle, pulled into the lazy Susan's movement as if I was on the tray myself, spinning and rotating through the world.

I rotated from China to America and then from Great Neck to Manhasset. Each spin sent me on another dizzying journey of adapting to new cultures and people. I was disappointed to learn while writing this essay that the sacred glass circle that I had treasured was instead reserved for summer barbecues here in America and actually had a name: Lazy Susan. The name sounded strange and unfamiliar, much like the rest of American culture. But although many things have changed and the crowning jewel of our New Year Celebration is no longer with us, my mom, my brother, and I always take the time to garnish our house with red lanterns, the Chinese character "fu," and a festive mood at the New Years. After all, the essence of the New Year is family and hope -- not just a rotatable glass plate.

My Perfect Plan to Become the President of the United States

This is part of a series of articles by Iris Liu, a rising sophomore attending Manhasset High School. Her goal is to inform the Chinese American community about the voting system and, as a result, encourage more people to vote in the upcoming general election.

As a child, the question you get asked most often is, "What are you going to be in the future?". Many of my friends struggle to find the answer to this question. There are simply too many components to consider. Their hobbies, their talents, and their desired income. But answering this question was never hard for me. As I, Iris Liu, can only be one thing and one thing only in the future: The President of The United States.

Of course, in order to become the President of The United States, I need to have the best possible plan, so detailed and advanced that there would be absolutely no doubt about me winning the election. Maybe you can help me out. Here it is:

My Plan to become President of the United States

On Election day, American citizens over the age of 18 can go to polling booths to cast their vote. The tally of the individual votes is the popular vote. But if you think all I need to do is win the majority of the votes, you're wrong! In 2016, Hillary Clinton received almost 3 million more votes than Donald Trump. But we all know who sits in the White House. So what happened? In three words: the electoral college.

This system is the actual judge for the presidential election, not the popular vote. In order for me to become the president, I will have to get the vote of at least 270 electors—more than half of all of them. Each state gets as many electors as it has members of congress and senators. New York has 27 members in the House of Representatives and two representatives in the Senate, so it gets 29 electors. I will win all 29 electoral votes if I win the popular vote in New York State. The catch is that even if I lose the majority vote by one vote in the state of New York, I will lose all 29 electoral votes. It is a winner take all situation, and no Electoral Votes will be split between my opponent and me.

It's important to remember, though, that the number of electors isn't proportional, state to state, to the number of voters. New York State has 19.5 million people. But Wyoming only has 578 thousand people, and yet they have three electoral votes. Let's do a quick math equation (don't worry, it's simple):

If we divide the total population of New York by the number of electors representing these people, we will get 672,413, which means that each elector in New York State represents a total of 672,413 people. However, if we run the calculation again for Wyoming, we will find that one elector in Wyoming actually represents 192,666 people.

Well, what does this mean? This means that if you vote in Wyoming, you have a greater influence over the results of the electoral votes than you do if you vote in New York. One elector represents fewer people in Wyoming, so one vote is worth a higher percentage of the total.

So now you might say, "Well, this seems unfair! Not only can the popular vote be pushed aside, some states even have an unfair advantage!" Well, the reasons why the founding fathers decided on the electoral college are pretty complicated, but if I get the chance, I'll write another article to introduce the origin of the electoral college.

The essential strategy every presidential candidate needs to understand is how to focus on campaigning in swing states instead of safe states. You see, there are states that tend to lean towards one political party. For example, New York skews heavily Democratic, and Texas skews Republican. These are called the "Safe States." These are the states that candidates like me won't go to for campaigning. While "Swing States are states that either a Republican or a Democrat can win. These are states I will focus my time and resources on.

Of course, I have a thorough understanding of this, and I fully applied it when the school announced that they would be using the Pass or Fail system. Immediately, I stopped spending 4 hours daily studying for my Math. I was already excelling in it, and there was no way I could fail the course. Why spend so much time? I gave up on Social Studies -- I could never understand the dreadfully boring topics and would fail regardless, so why bother? Instead, I put all my attention into Science, the course that has an upcoming AP exam. I might be failing now, but with a little work, I can pass the class.

(Ok, I'm just kidding. As a child whose parents are very strict about me getting straight A's, I have to be careful what I say or get disowned by my family).

Now let's talk about my fabulous plan for how to completely dominate the competition in the primary elect-oh, hold on. I just remembered something. In order to run for office, you have to be a natural-born citizen! I can't believe it. After all that work, too? That really is disappointing. Well, hopefully, at least my research will help you understand the electoral system better. Who knows, maybe one day you can use this knowledge to run for President! If you succeed, don't forget to mention me!

Open Letter to the Chinese Community

Nonfiction

Part 1 of 5 articles originally published by LICAA in Chinese and English in the summer of 2020. Writing and Translation by Iris Liu.

Chinese Americans have suffered from varying degrees of discrimination and racial stereotypes. We are the model minority. We are responsible for COVID-19. We do math very well. We are silent, content sheep in a chaotic world, satisfied with our lot in life. But this is far from the truth. We can be very vocal about our political leanings and beliefs, from serious issues like the morality of the death sentence to everyday problems like what type of flour is best for making sponge cake. Sure, some of us are not U.S. citizens and do not have the right to vote in elections. Those people feel disengaged: why would anyone, after all, buy cake and ice cream for a party that they are not allowed to attend? However, many Chinese Americans are citizens and still choose not to vote. This is maddening because if our engagement on WeChat is any indication--endless streams of all-caps passion--we have plenty of thoughts about the direction of the country. I decided to write this letter, then, because I have grown tired of people in the Chinese community quarreling about politics and yet doing nothing to change the problems they complain about. We must vote.

Although the Asian-American community is the fastest-growing demographic of eligible voters in the United States, only 47 percent of Asian-Americans vote, compared to 66 percent of black voters and 64 percent of non-Hispanic white voters. To make matters worse, only 41 percent of eligible Chinese-Americans vote. We are the least likely to vote by percentage among all Asian Americans. Such a low percentage of votes lessens the influence of Chinese Americans in social and political affairs. Political parties will sacrifice our community's interests in exchange for more political power. To change this situation, Chinese-Americans must take action right now, starting with the upcoming primary election on June 23rd. This year's primary is particularly special. Generally speaking, in the primary election, pre-registered Republican and Democratic voters vote for the presidential candidates they support for their respective parties. But this year's Republican primary was canceled, with support thrown towards incumbent Donald Trump. The Democratic Primary was delayed due to the epidemic. Later, as the other candidates withdrew from the campaign, the New York Board of Elections voted to cancel the Democratic Primary, which would have effectively given the victory to Biden, citing a new state law that allows the Board of Electors to remove candidates from the ballot if they publicly announce that they're dropping from the race. They felt this would save time, money, and, most importantly, lives. However, the primaries are about far more than just selecting the future American president. By staying on the ballot, candidates can receive more delegates to the Democratic National Convention this summer and thus increase their influence over the party's policies.

    Candidate Andrew Yang understood the importance of the primary election. He filed a lawsuit soon after the board announced the cancellation of this year's primaries. The lawsuit argued that by removing candidates from the ballot, voters would lose their first amendment right, the freedom of speech. Bernie Sanders joined Andrew Yang, supporting the measure to reinstate the elections. Together they argued that this primary provides a crucial opportunity for voters to express their support for politicians and policies. In addition, the primaries will decide the number of pledged delegates that each candidate will bring to the National convention in August. Their efforts reversed the work of the Board of Electors, and the Democratic primary is now again scheduled for this coming Tuesday.

The rights to a primary this year that Andrew Yang and Bernie Sanders fought for is a significant opportunity for the Chinese-American community to make a difference. By voting, you are showing respect for yourself and for the system that we are living under. More importantly, by voting for politicians that stand with policies you agree with, you are giving these politicians the power to change the course of the government and thus shape America's future. One vote is better than typing a thousand words on Wechat. So I strongly urge all of my community to unite and take action immediately.

Chapter 3

Experimentation & Reflection Leads to Progress

(Tenth grade)

Dream Baker

Fantasy Story - published on Teen Ink

Sylvia hummed along to the gentle tune flowing out of the radio as she carefully weighed the flour in a dainty golden cup. On the table, she laid out her usual ingredients: a rose made out of butter, a singing lemon, and of course, some cheesy sugar.

From the corner of the kitchen, a small shadow slipped into the room. Upon first glance, the figure appeared to be a small cat, But it was translucent and flickered in and out of focus like a bad television signal.

"Hi, Baku!" Sylvia peeked up from her work. "What do you have for me?"

Baku leaped up to the kitchen counter. Small flickering yellow orbs were spinning around his tail as if he was pulling them along his body with a string.

"Let's see here...a memory about Lin's first hike, a jar of sand from her favorite beach, oh and a picture of a cloud shaped like an apple. Very nice, Baku. This might be one of your best excursions yet!"

Sylvia softly scratched Baku's ears, earning a pleased purr. His fur was the color of heavy whipped cream except for one spot on the top of his forehead where it turned to black, which looked like someone had carelessly tipped a jar of ink right onto the creature's head. Baku's eyes were soft and gentle, much like swirled frosting on top of a cupcake.

Sylvia immediately got to work. Opening up the cabinets, she pulled out jars of glowing lights and a huge silver bowl the size of her torso.

"Well," she said to Baku, "I think with the ingredients you brought back today, we can make something really exciting! Maybe... a dream about flying! How about that?"

Of course, Sylvia didn't expect Baku to answer, but it's not really like she has anyone else to talk to within the kitchen. It was a part of her job to stay in here, but that didn't mean she couldn't make it more fun for herself. She took the memory of Lin's first hike and threw it into the bowl, along with one handful of sugar, a spoon of lemon zest, the picture of an apple-shaped cloud, and finally, something that would bring the whole cake together: some delight. To Sylvia, delight smelled like apples, plums, and yogurt, her three favorite foods.

Sylvia sprinkled a glowing substance from one of the jars into the gigantic bowl. Immediately, the bowl flew into the air, trembling as the aroma of lemon, dew, and firewood swarmed the room.

Sylvia's eyes shone with excitement as she stared at the floating bowl. It was almost like she herself was slowly shifting into Lin's dream, flying through the clouds with a smile so bright it hurt her face, feeling the sunshine brushing against her skin.

"Now it's time to change it up!" She beamed at Baku.

The diligent baker rushed from one cabinet to the next, gliding like a dancer as she pulled out all kinds of ingredients: phoenix feathers to create a set of wings for Lin and a memory of the young girl visiting Big Ben. As the dream baker tossed each ingredient into the bowl, a ray of blinding light shot out.

Sylvia always put great effort into everything she created, even when Baku brought back ingredients that were less than ideal for her vision. Like that memory of the one time when Lin fought with her parents about eating pig's feet or one where a mean girl made fun of the shape of her eyes. Those couldn't possibly be made into a dream! Dreams were supposed to be happy, pleasant confections that helped the dreamer sleep comfortably. Sylvia wouldn't be a good baker if she let sadness and anger slip into the cake mix.

After the amount of time it takes to make a lemon sing, the bowl stopped shaking. When it landed, all the ingredients were gone. The only thing left was the scents of dew and firewood still lingering in the air. Sylvia grabbed the bowl and peeked inside: the dream was a success! As per usual, of course. She spun her fingers, and the cake flew from the bowl and onto one of the counters.

Sylvia called for Baku and began to put the ingredients back into the designated cabinets. Baku hurried down the stairs and leaped onto the counter with joy.

"Time for dinner, bud!" She loved watching him eat the dreams she'd created.

Baku unhinged his jaw, and it dropped all the way onto the counter. His fangs grew larger, and his pupils dilated before he suddenly swallowed the whole cake at once. Buttercream got smeared on his whiskers and coat, but he didn't seem to mind. He hopped down from the counter and curled himself into a corner. Without Baku, Sylvia wouldn't have any ingredients and a way to deliver the dreams to Lin. Plus, he is pretty good company.

Every day, Sylvia wakes up just as the sun starts to climb down from the sky, bakes a dream with a new and fun concept, and goes to rest when Lin wakes up the next morning. Over the next few days, she baked a cake about Lin meeting her idol, a boy singer with gelled hair spikes and eyeshadow, a cake about a giant tiger named Phu, and a cake about painting a lovely meadow in Brazil. Her life was slow, but she never found it boring.

But a few days later, when Baku returned from his trip, there weren't any glowing orbs surrounding him.

"What's wrong?" Sylvia asked. Baku looked like he had been tossed into the washing machine. His hair was sticking out in all different directions. He threw himself into a metal pot and refused to budge.

The dream baker tried to coax him out of the pot with some leftover dough, but Baku only hissed at her before burying himself deeper. Maybe that last cake had given him a stomach ache, she thought. It happened once in a while. With a sigh, she decided to make do with leftovers for Lin's dream that night. Using crushed amethysts, some chopped-up memories about a late summer night, and a jar of preserved fireflies, Sylvia baked a basic dream about Lin having a picnic with her friends. Baku sniffed the cake. He didn't seem happy, but he was hungry. That was a good sign. He ate the cake and went to sleep in his favorite corner.

The next morning before Baku left for his trip, Sylvia made sure to get up and say goodbye. "Baku, I really need you to try to bring some ingredients back today, okay? The leftovers are all gone. I don't want you to starve."

But when Baku came back that night, he looked as if he had seen a ghost, and he again brought no new ingredients for Sylvia. He again curled up in his favorite metal pot. Sylvia pondered why Baku looked so down--he was usually a happy cat. Had he been nibbling on bad memories again?

"Baku, dear. You have to go out. Without ingredients, I can't bake. Lin needs to dream!"

But Baku refused to budge. Sylvia was worried, but she had an important job to do. She picked up her cat. But as soon as she grabbed the door handle to send him on his way, Baku let out a cry of despair and hooked his claws into the walls in a desperate attempt to escape back into his pot.

"Come on, Baku!" Sylvia tugged against his claws, trying to make him let go of the wall. "If you go, I'll bake you a special peanut butter cookie. I know they're your favorite!"

Baku meowed in complaint and dug his claws even deeper into the wood. Sylvia didn't want to pull on his arms too hard, so the two stood at the doorway in a stalemate. Finally defeated, Sylvia relaxed her grip on Baku; he quickly wriggled out from her clutches and ran to safety underneath the couch. He meowed plaintively.

"I'm sorry, alright?" Sylvia crossed her arms over her chest and groaned. "How am I supposed to do my job if there is nothing to bake?"

"Or..." She suddenly had an idea and sat down crossed-legged on the floor. She'd have to go out by herself. It was her only choice, even though she had no know idea where all of Lin's memories were stored. In fact, she'd never taken one step outside her kitchen in her entire life. Sylvia grew anxious thinking about the possibilities of the outside world. But if a pastry-loving cat could do it, so could she.

She leaned down next to the couch where Baku was hiding. "You rest until you feel better," she said. "I'll do your job for now." Baku poked his head out and stared at Sylvia. She patted him on the head and decided that she had to be strong so that Baku wouldn't worry.

The next day, Sylvia woke up before the moon. Her kitchen was eerily silent and empty without any music playing or any baking supplies out; it was as if there were invisible eyes staring at her. She began to pack her bags with jars for ingredients. Then her foot started to jitter nervously like an over-caffeinated squirrel. Hunting for memories scared her. What if she got lost?

The few steps to the door seemed to take forever. Once there, she stood staring at the metal doorknob that glistened like an invitation and the wooden patterns of the door. She couldn't move for a moment. She took a deep breath, finally, and mustered the courage to open the door.

Everything was pitch black; the darkness was like a bottomless pit that threatened to swallow her whole. She carefully took a tentative step and was met with a soft carpet-like sensation underneath her pink sneakers. Sylvia braced herself--she was doing this for Lin!--and dashed forward.

Green and brown leaves spilled across the field, beneath her feet, miles of grass expanded into the horizon; all around were trees with bent and twisted trunks. The air smelled like a musty library. The branches that shot up to the sky were braided together to form a twisted blanket, blocking out most of the sunlight except for little bits that slipped through.

Sylvia stared in bewilderment. The little bubble that was her whole world had suddenly expanded to miles of undiscovered land, and she couldn't help but think of how beautiful everything was. Yet, she knew that it wasn't this beautiful landscape that deterred Baku. It must've been something else much more dangerous. A chill ran up her spine.

After some time walking, a bright flash of white light zoomed through the trees. Sylvia followed the light to a hanging branch under a rotting tree, thinking that the light was a memory. Yet what she saw was something terrifying. The creature didn't have any flesh on its face, just a glowing white skull that looked part chicken and part dragon. Sharp fangs protruded from its jaw. Black goo, stinking of rotten eggs, dripped down on both sides of the monster's head. The body of the creature resembled a monkey's and was almost twice the size of Sylvia, but it had a human arm for a tail; the human hand attached to it flailed around wildly.

Sylvia screamed as she studied the horrible creature. She suddenly wished she had brought her rolling pin for self-defense. Although she hadn't known what to expect when she went out to find what had scared Baku, she hadn't expected anything like this: the most ferocious creature imaginable.

The creature then roared. It sounded like a human baby's cries; cold spikes of fear pushed into Sylvia's heart. The monster flared its teeth and examined her with hollow eyes. Sylvia's hands immediately went to her ears as she tried to back slowly away.

But the creature lurched out of the tree with terrifying speed and leaped at Sylvia. She threw herself to the side just in time and narrowly avoided being ripped to shreds. Before the creature could get up, Sylvia scrambled for cover and ran.

The creature turned and then snarled at Sylvia. And then, with its huge jaw hanging open, scurried after her. Sylvia ran frantically as she leaped over fallen trunks of wood and scattered rocks. She dashed into a thicket of neck-high bushes on her left, hoping that the monster would lose track of her. Somehow, in spite of the tangle of thorns and branches, she kept running.

The creature growled unhappily. It used its sharp claws to climb up a nearby tree where it was able to see her running; it grabbed onto a branch that hung above the bushes. Using its human arm-like tail, it swung itself between trees and quickly closed the distance between them.

Sylvia looked through her small backpack for anything she could use to slow down the monster, anything at all. Her heart drilled against her ribcage, trying to escape her body. Her little kitchen had always been comforting and safe. This was the first time in Sylvia's life she'd ever felt true fear.

She pulled two jars out of her backpack. It seemed unlikely she could hurt the creature with them, but they were the only weapons she had. Sylvia turned her body towards the approaching monster. With one hand, she aimed the first jar at the creature's head and flung it as hard as she could at the monster. The jar whizzed right past its head and crashed into a tree. And the creature kept coming.

With nothing to lose, Sylvia yelled as loud as she could. "GO AWAY!"

To her surprise, the creature stopped in its tracks and even backed off a few steps. It then shrieked so horrifically that the sharp noise almost made Sylvia pass out. But she forced herself to relax and control her breath. She had to keep her senses. The creature started creeping forward again. One step. Closer.

And closer. As fast Sylvia could, she threw the other jar with all her might.

"AAARGH!!" The monster screamed in pain as the jar cracked against its tail. Its fingers curled into a fist as it spasmed. The tail fell, and it hung limply against its side. Sylvia's eyes widened. She was gonna get out of this mess, after all. But before she could start running again, the creature grabbed onto her. Sylvia could feel the claws tightening on her shoulder and turned to look at the creature. She closed her eyes and braced herself, waiting for the claws to rip her apart, but the monster simply cradled her in its arms. She opened her eyes, and all she saw was its empty skull staring back at her. Why hadn't it killed her yet?

Sylvia broke out of her trance and realized she still had one of the jars in her right hand. She reached up and slammed it on the creature's head. It shattered, and the monster fell backward, releasing her.

RUN! She screamed to herself while stumbling over roots and rocks. *FASTER!*

But she'd been running for too long, and her knees began to buckle. Sweat and tears flowed together on her face as her despair grew. Just how was she going to get out of this? Then, beneath her feet, the color of the plain grass started to change color like a chameleon. At first, it looked like specks of red paint flung onto a green canvas, but as Sylvia ran deeper and deeper into the forest, the red began to swallow everything in sight. Even the trees began to drip with bright red paint; it reminded Sylvia of the red envelopes full of money Lin would receive during the Chinese New Year.

"What is going on?" Sylvia whispered.

Behind her, the monster started to jitter nervously and glanced down to the ground. It grew slower in its pursuit, yet it still snarled at Sylvia with its jagged teeth. Sylvia continued running in spite of the pain burning her legs, speeding through the red leaves and branches.

She burst into an open field with a twisting tree in the center. The tree was about five times the size of her own house, twisting yellow vines nestled on the branches like glowing veins. Sylvia sped past through the grass and ran into the field before turning back at the scream behind her.

"ARRRGHHH!" The monster behind her gave a frustrated yell. It sat down at the border of the red grass field, growling unhappily as it picked at the grass beneath it.

"Ok, so there is something here," Sylvia mumbled to herself in confirmation. She wiped the sweat on her palms with her pants and nervously adjusted her shoes. She hesitantly stepped deeper into the field while glancing back at the monster. One step. Two steps. This place didn't seem particularly threatening. Waves of wind brushed against her hair. Sunlight pierced through the red leaves, illuminating the field in inviting light. But Sylvia knew better than to let her guard down.

"Why are you here?" A sharp voice called out.

Sylvia jumped in surprise and frantically looked for the source of the voice.

"Who is that?" she asked tentatively.

A muffled voice seemed to be coming from the center of the tree trunk. Sylvia moved closer.

Even though the voice sounded annoyed, at least it didn't sound like it wanted to devour her. "Can you help me?" She asked. "I'm being chased by this terrible monster. I don't know if you have any idea what it is, but it seems to be scared of this tree. Can you please let me hide until it goes away?"

The creature paced back and forth on the edge of the field, still grumbling.

She heard a whisper coming from inside the trunk. "What...no, we are not...insane."

Sylvia, confused by this response, scratched her head. Sharp whispers and deep grunts coming from the inside of the tree got louder and more panicked. Sylvia heard a few phrases and squeaks; it sounded like an out-of-tune chorus of mice screaming inside the tree.

"Please! I'm really scared. I don't have anything to defend myself with. I promise I won't harm you!"

More indistinct whispers came drifting out of the trunk: "Harumph... some people have all the nerve... missing Wheel of Fortune." Finally, there was a heavy sigh. "Fine."

With a mouse-like squeak, the side of the tree transformed into a door. Tiny golden strung-together bulbs dropped out of the canopy, spelling out a blocky "welcome."

"Come in now," the voice grumbled. "Remember to take off your shoes."

"Oh yes, thank you so much." Sylvia took off her shoes and stepped into the door.

The inside of the tree was hollowed out all the way to an open, blue sky. The walls were carved into rows of bookshelves all the way up and around the trunk, so high and so many that she got dizzy trying to count them all. The books--there must have been millions--all seemed to be made out of either rock, paper, or scissors. Each shelf had a label. Sylvia looked to the shelf on the left that said "kindergarten."

But most shocking of all were the creatures that ran the place. They looked like tiny origami people a child would cut out of paper. And even though they were only as tall as Sylvia's ankle, they were surprisingly strong. A group of them carried stacks of papers from one shelf to another. Suddenly, one turned itself into an origami bird and flew to the very top of a shelf labeled Family and began looking through the books stacked there. And three other origami people peeked at her behind the legs of a middle-aged gentleman.

He looked to be around forty years old and had a grim, cold face that stood out from the warm and busy atmosphere of the room. His shirt was ironed perfectly and fitted around him seamlessly. His hair was greased back, and he wore stiff dress pants and perfectly shined polka dot shoes that changed from black and white every time Sylvia blinked. Yet this well-kept together exterior only made the eyebags beneath his eyes and the single strand of hair dangling on his forehead that much more noticeable.

"Hello," The man spoke with slight disdain, glaring at her from head to toe. Sylvia shifted uncomfortably.

"You are Sylvia, the dream baker." The man said, tugging a strand of loose hair behind his ear only for it to bounce back immediately. "Why aren't you at your station? We cannot afford errors to the system, and if you're not properly situated in Unconsciousness Sector 3, the human host will quickly become insomniac."

"I'm very sorry," Sylvia smiled sheepishly, feeling restless after hearing what could happen to Lin. "But my cat stopped bringing back ingredients for dreams. So I needed to come out and find some myself."

The old man furrowed his brow. "Ah. Of course. I bet Chaos was keeping Baku from doing his job." At the sight of her confused stare, he added, "Chaos is the name we have chosen for the creature that was trying to catch you."

Well, that was certainly not good news. Sylvia was reminded that she would have to cross the forest yet again to get back to her home. What would she do if she encountered Chaos again?

She must not have disguised her fear very well because the man coughed lightly to get her attention again.

"No dreams. This is very bad," the old man said. "We must solve this. Yes, we must." He scratched his nose. Just as Sylvia was about to speak, he asked, "Is there anything else you know about what's happening? Something that might have provoked Chaos?"

"Well..." Sylvia thought about it but couldn't think of anything. "No. Except for that creature, everything has been perfectly fine." She felt her face get red with embarrassment. She wished she could offer more. "Do you know how I can get away from him?"

"Get away from him?" The man looked puzzled; the origami people hiding behind his leg poked their heads out. "Why do you want to do that?"

"Because he's trying to kill me?" Sylvia asked in disbelief.

"Chaos isn't violent." The man clapped twice, and one of the origami people folded themselves into a bird, picked up a red folder from a box in its beak, and dropped it onto Sylvia's hands. She fumbled with the folder before opening it. The papers inside contained an illustration of Chaos along with stacks of printed paper.

"Look." The man waddled over and pointed to some writing that had been circled with a red pen. "Our records here specifically state that Chaos is harmless. Although Chaos creatures may appear intimidating, it is only because they are born out of suppressed desires."

Sylvia sighed. "Well, I'm surprised to hear that. I almost died out there!" She paused to think for a moment. None of this made any sense. "Besides," she said, "I would know if Lin had any suppressed memories."

"Actually," the man said. "You wouldn't. This is where all of Lin's thoughts, memories, and emotions are stored." He pointed to the shelves, looking very pleased with himself. "In fact, this is where your little buddy, Baku, gets the ingredients for your dream cakes. He has made himself quite comfortable with our employees here."

At the sound of Baku's name, all the origami people and birds dropped what they were doing and squeaked in excitement. They unfolded themselves into pieces of paper as a gentle breeze swooped down and lifted them into the air. They swirled and fluttered until they formed a giant replica of Baku.

Sylvia watched the transformation of the origami people with awe and didn't even realize her jaw was open until one of the origami people landed on top of her head. Slowly, she looked around and approached a shelf on her left labeled eight-year-old. It was stacked with books made out of paper, rock, and scissors that ranged from colors of pink, turquoise, gray, and yellow. The shelf itself was quite worn, littered with crayon doodles and scratch marks.

She pulled out a yellow paper book and opened it to a random page. Instantly, three yellow orbs flew out of the paper and hovered next to her, displaying memories of Lin's first bike ride, her favorite childhood dessert, and a picture of Lin making a friendship bracelet.

"Well..." Sylvia closed the book and put it back in its place. These memories really do look identical to the ones that Baku brings home. "Then if she does have these suppressed desires, can't you just look at your records, find out what it is, and then kinda un-suppress it?"

"When a memory is suppressed," the old man said, "not even we can help Baku find it."

The man raised an eyebrow and rolled his eyes. "We're all part of Lin's consciousness. If she's hiding something, none of us would know. Just like how some memories here are eroded because Lin forgot about them. How to face Chaos is something that you'll have to figure out yourself."

"Me?"

"Please stop making me repeat myself."

"I'm just in charge of baking cakes. I'm not some warrior that can slay the monster!"

The man groaned and rubbed his eyes. "For the last time, Chaos will not harm you. If it is chasing you, there's a good reason! You are the only station in the emotional subconscious branch that can directly interfere with Lin's thoughts. Now go and do your job." He turned and started to leave.

"What, wait, hold on!" While Sylvia was trying to make sense of the conversation, the origami people unfolded themselves from the Giant Baku formation and transformed into a giant crane.

The man stood by, idly pushing down an unruly strand of his hair. "A word of warning. Don't run away from Chaos. He really doesn't like that." He clapped twice. The tree branches, in response, pulled apart to reveal a round hole just big enough for the crane to fly through. The giant paper bird gently picked Sylvia up with its beak and flew through the hole. Red leaves fluttered past them, and as they flew higher and higher, the tree grew smaller and smaller in the distance until all that was left was a tiny red dot.

"That guy was very rude," Sylvia said into the wind, and then, scared for a moment she would fall, clutched onto the crane's mouth as she tried not to stare at the carpet of endless white clouds beneath her feet. After a few sweeps of the crane's giant paper wings, it began to make a slow descent.

The creature dropped Sylvia on a patch of soft grass right in front of her kitchen. The crane tucked its wings and landed next to her as it nuzzled her with its beak. She giggled and gently patted the crane's head, whispering thanks. Then the creature spread its wings and leaped into the air as Sylvia looked with amazement at how it flew so effortlessly into the sky.

Sylvia scrambled to her feet and rushed inside. With a loud bang, she slammed the door shut behind her and called out for Baku.

"Baku! Baku, come here!"

"Meow?" The fluffy white cat scurried from a corner and leaped into Sylvia's arms.

"Oh, you will not believe the day I've had today. All that work, and I didn't get a single new ingredient!" Sylvia rubbed her face against Baku's soft fur, feeling relieved at a familiar presence after a day of so much excitement and conflict.

Baku purred like a motor engine and licked Sylvia's hands to comfort her. Sylvia plopped herself down on her sofa and thought about what to do next. The librarian said that Lin would slowly become an insomniac if Sylvia didn't take action, so she needed to do something fast.

But what? Sylvia clicked her tongue. She was just a baker and didn't know how to deal with Lin's suppressed desires, whatever those were.

"Oh, wait!" Sylvia yelped, causing Baku to jump away. "I am just a Baker! But the librarian said that the Chaos came to me for a reason, so it must be related to something that only I could do - baking dreams!"

She sat up and scanned through all the dreams she'd ever baked. There was one where Lin was transformed into a fantasy world where she defeated a dragon--How FUN!--and this one about Lin having a magical tea party with some talking cats--Delightful! She was sure all her dreams were perfect. But Baku meowed very loudly, and suddenly she remembered there was one dream in particular that didn't go well. And it was a dream from just before all this trouble.

She'd accidentally included a bad memory from a family dinner party. Lin's mom had brought up a plate of steaming cooked pig's feet, mentioning as she always did that it was good for the skin. Lin didn't think twice. She'd eaten pig's feet, duck blood, and cow tongues since she was a child. But her friend, Alice, who was visiting to work on their history project, coiled away in disgust. She whispered to Lin, "That food is so unsanitary. Your family is gross." Lin immediately agreed with her and refused to eat the dish that night, much to her mother's chagrin.

It was a memory that caused a lot of confusion and disgust in Lin's heart, and although Sylvia hadn't included all of the memory in her recipe, the baking bowl that night had puked out a gross lump of dripping, slime-like substance. Then the very next day, Baku came home without any ingredients.

"That can't be a coincidence." Sylvia decided to recreate that cake. It was the only way she could think to figure out what had caused Chaos to appear. In fact, she would make the worst cake she'd ever made in her life.

She grabbed all the bad memories that she'd refused to use in her recipes over the years: one about a girl who called Lin's lunch from home "stinky" and another about a girl on the playground making fun of the shape of Lin's eyes. And then, with a swish, Sylvia poured in the pig's feet memory. At first, nothing happened, and Sylvia sulked, wondering if she would ever be able to bake dreams ever again. But then, the bowl, under its own power, flew up into the air and shook with an intensity that Sylvia had never seen before.

It felt like all the air in the kitchen was being sucked into the bowl. Then it stopped shaking and exploded with a loud BAM! When the bowl floated down, a container made from bamboo lay peacefully inside, radiating an enticing aroma.

Sylvia reached out and lifted up the lid on the top. And there it was, a pair of pig's feet. Just as fresh as Sylvia had remembered seeing in Lin's memories. A honey-like sauce drizzled over them, making them shine like gems under the light.

She suddenly heard a loud thump from outside the door. With a jolt, she leaped towards the narrow window and peered outside. A gray shadow swung between the trees, screaming and scratching at everything in sight as it approached the kitchen.

"Chaos." Sylvia braced herself.

The creature quickly dashed to the house and smashed its skull against the window. It let out a horrible scream as its body suddenly inflated to thrice its size. The fangs on its skull grew sharper and longer, and it raised its arm-like tail far above its head and then, with a whoosh, smashed through the window! Shards of glass flew everywhere.

Sylvia covered her head instinctively. When she looked up again, she found that the creature held Baku in its now giant hand.

Gray clouds rolled in from a distance and blocked the few rays of sunlight leaking from the knitted branches. Sylvia looked on from the broken window and saw that the trees around the field in front of her house were now twisting and pulsing with black mucus-like slime. In the center of the field, Chaos stood; it had grown so tall that it looked like it could touch the sky. Its tail was still waving around and held poor Baku. Sylvia's heart lurched at the sight; she needed to act fast.

She grabbed the pig's feet and walked outside. "Here, Chaos!" Sylvia slowly crouched down and placed the bamboo container on the ground. "Eat this, and you'll feel better!".

Chaos sniffed the air. Its eyes lit up with recognition. Slowly, it turned its hideous skull and dripping liquid body around and dropped Baku onto the ground, trodding toward Sylvia.

It stopped right before the container and bent down to examine it. When it opened the lid with its large claws, it let out a thunderous scream that shook the ground.

Chaos then tilted its head with curiosity as it rapidly began to shrink. After only a minute, it had shrunk to half Sylvia's size. Whatever she was doing, it was working! Chaos leaned closer to the food, its eyes shining with hunger. Finally, it grabbed the pig's feet with its fangs and gobbled one of them down in a few bites. Licking its teeth and lying down,

Unbecoming

Chaos purred in satisfaction before starting to delicately eat the other one.

As it ate, its human-hand tail transformed into a furry black tail. Its skull transformed into something that resembled a cat's, and its body solidified into licorice-like fur.

"You're actually kind of cute!" Sylvia exclaimed.

Chaos finally finished eating its pig's feet and finished his transformation. Sylvia allowed herself to collapse onto the grass in exhaustion and called for Baku.

Striding over, Baku greeted his new friend with a meow and fitted himself into Sylvia's arms.

"Aw, I missed you too." She petted her pal.

Chaos placed his paw on top of Sylvia's and chirped in an apologetic manner.

"It's ok, bud." Sylvia scratched his chin. "That was a tough adventure, but I'm glad I was able to help Lin. But man, that friend of hers, Alice, is so mean! Lin should get a new friend!"

Chaos and Baku meowed in response.

After the stand-off with Chaos, the origami people and the librarian came to visit Sylvia on a sunny afternoon. They gave her a polished diary along with a beautiful orange fountain pen to keep her busy mind calm.

Sylvia was still a bit upset about the way the Librarian had left Sylvia to figure out what to do about Chaos by herself. But after spending more time with him, she began to realize he only wanted what was best for Lin. She still kind of hated his habit of talking in riddles and snapping at her, but she saw he was a good man with a big heart.

When Sylvia went into the kitchen to get more lemonade for her guests, she looked down and saw something precious: Baku and Chaos were curled around each other. They were so tightly wound, in fact, that they looked like one creature, half black, half white; they now resembled a Chinese symbol that she'd seen many times in Lin's memories. The yin/yang.

Family Dinner

Drama Script - Scholastics Honorable Mention

Characters

It's morning, and ZELLE is cooking in her kitchen. Jars of spices are aligned on the shelf, labeled with messy Chinese letters. The fan above the stove buzzes as it sucks up smoke from the sizzling pan. Zelle, 54, is pushing around potstickers on the pan. She appears older than she is, with small wrinkles lining her features. She wears a red apron wrapped around her waist.

OWEN, 23, wears a neatly pressed dress shirt and pants. He exits his bedroom and greets his mother, walking with determination and purpose.

                    OWEN
Morning.

                    ZELLE
You're up early.

                    OWEN
Yeah, the administrator said I should deliver the results as soon as possible.

                    ZELLE
But you haven't even eaten breakfast!

OWEN
I'm not hungry.

ZELLE
I'm cooking potstickers.

OWEN
Ma, all you cook are potstickers.

ZELLE
Just sit down.

OWEN
I have to get to the airport by 8:30.

ZELLE
I know that, but breakfast will take fifteen minutes max.

OWEN
Oh fine.
    (Owen sits)

ZELLE
Have some vegetables and pour some vinegar for yourself.

    (Owen pulls two plates of potstickers over. Zelle sits too; both of them grab their chopsticks and start to eat.)

ZELLE
Last night I had a dream.

OWEN
About what?

ZELLE
I dreamed that you decided to move back to New York.

OWEN
Ok.

ZELLE
You'd grown to seven feet tall. You were an absolute giant. And you and I and your dad planted a garden together full of apple trees. You could reach the tallest branches and pull them down for us.

OWEN
It's only a dream, ma.

ZELLE
What?

OWEN
I'm not a giant. I'm just me. I like my job. It's exciting, and the pay's great.

ZELLE
But you live so far away.

OWEN
It's not that far.

ZELLE
There's no one to take care of you in Austin.

OWEN
I'm an adult. I can care for myself.

ZELLE
And there's a job opening in your father's office too. Isn't that perfect?

OWEN
Are you even listening to me?

ZELLE
I just don't get what's so good about that place that you'd leave your family for it.

(Owen takes a bite of the potstickers)

ZELLE
Well?

OWEN
I should be able to do whatever I want. I don't need to give you a reason.

ZELLE
Oh! So now you're talking back to me.

OWEN
I just don't want to.

ZELLE
We have provided for you your entire life. Now that you've got a new job, will you leave us?

OWEN
I'm not leaving you.

ZELLE
I don't see what's the difference when you never even call.

OWEN
Listen. This is the exact reason why I never call.

ZELLE
I'm just a mother caring for her son. Owen, do you have any idea how hard it is to move to another city alone?

OWEN
I've been there for three months already, and I have already made friends.

ZELLE
It's your father's birthday next Monday. Can you at least come back for that? It would mean so much to him.

OWEN
I'll try, but a lot is going on in my life right now.

ZELLE
But can't you at least make it to your father's birthday?

OWEN
Can you just stop? (to himself) Man.

(Zelle turns.)

ZELLE
(angrily)

Soon I'll be too old to walk and take care of myself. Where will you be then? I fed you, raised you, and gave everything I had, but you grew up and still avoid your family like the plague. I'm your mother, Owen!

(Owen throws his chopsticks down)

OWEN
You know what? I can't take your childish behavior anymore. All you do is tell me, *"Do this, Owen, oh no, you can't do that. You are too young to know anything."* I've grown up. Can't you see that?

ZELLE
No. You will always be my precious son. You don't understand.

(Owen doesn't reply and grabs his jacket from the chair, slamming the door behind him.)

(Zelle sighs, sitting back down at the dinner table. She pulls over the plate and bites into the potsticker. Something about it doesn't taste right. She pushes it away and looks towards the door.)

(Blackout.)

END OF PLAY

The Obstacle Course

Personal Narrative - Round 4 Finalist NYT Personal Narrative Contest

My brother repositioned himself at the starting line: the couch. We glared at each other like the sworn enemies we were. It was a battle for glory and the right to the last bag of barbecue-flavored chips--everything was on the line.

We dashed past the TV playing news of the day, the giant clay pot that contained colorful goldfish, and toward the finish line--the balcony.

Just then, a voice cut through our screams.

"What do you think you're doing?"

Turning around, I saw Gugu (Chinese for aunt). Her brows were frowning so hard they distorted the air around her.

"I hope I didn't hear those monkey noises coming out of my Tiantian." She pursed her lips. "And your hair is all over the place. So unladylike!" My aunt leaned closer. The smell of her perfume was suffocating.

Gugu always had a well-assembled bun on the top of her head, neatly ironed ankle-length dresses, and never seemed happy with how I acted. Yet she never said a word about my brother's bad posture or the socks thrown all over his bedroom.

She twisted her jade rings. "Never do this obstacle course again. Promise?"

I wanted to scream and make her understand that I loved the obstacle course game. But I didn't scream. I wanted her approval.

"I promise," I said.

"Good girl." She nodded and walked away.

As soon as Gugu was out of sight, I ran into the bathroom and looked at myself in the mirror. I was out of breath, and my eyes were red. I raised a pair of golden fabric scissors I'd found in the sewing box underneath my mom's bed. In my mind, being a boy meant having short hair, and I didn't want to be a girl anymore if it meant having so many burdens.

One clump fell onto the floor, then another. I saw my reflection in the mirror looking more and more like a boy, and I felt lighter and freer.

When my parents got home from the movies, they were shocked. But they calmly sat me down on the couch and asked me why I'd done it. My frustrations bubbled in my throat, but they wouldn't form into words. I cowered underneath my parents' fierce gaze and cracked my knuckles one by one.

They let me off with the promise that I wouldn't use scissors without permission again

Later that night, my brother knocked on my door.

"Here." He handed me the bag of barbeque-flavored chips--the obstacle course prize. My brother's eyes were red too. "I'm sorry I took the chips from you."

"You didn't take them. You won them fair and square."

"But you're the girl, and the boy should always *rang zhe* the girl. *Rang zhe* translates roughly to "prioritize."

I realized that if my brother was saying this, then short hair didn't mean freedom at all. We're all bound by these rules. My parents had obviously forced him to come into my room.

I pictured myself running the obstacle course. I felt so free. And freedom, I realized, was more than the length of your hair or the shape of your body. Freedom was the choices you made on your own.

"No," I said to my brother as I thought about growing my hair out again. "I don't think you're right about that."

I handed the chips back.

An Open Letter to the Educational Department of New York State

Research Paper

Written to send to Legislators and Assemblymembers

On August 8, 1785, the first three documented Chinese men, Ashing, Achun, and Aceun, arrived in Baltimore aboard the ship *Pallas* and were stranded after their ship captain unexpectedly retired from further voyages.[1] Since then, 14.1 million Asian immigrants have settled in the United States.[2] Despite our contributions to the economy, culture, and politics of the country, we have been used as scapegoats for conflicts and crises while our real history is ignored by the New York State U.S. history curriculum. I am frustrated and disheartened by this, particularly in light of the recent rise in Asian hate crimes. While progressive movements and protests have brought advancements in the struggle for equality in the United States, the increase of hate and violence towards Asian Americans over the past two years makes it clear that the problem of racial discrimination is far from over. Poor education has, at the least, been one reason for these crimes.

The racial scapegoating of Asian Americans can be traced back to the very expansion of the nation

---

[1] "SCSU Research Guides: Chinese-Americans 1785-: Home," SCSU Research Guides at Southern Connecticut State University, accessed on May 21, 2021, https://libguides.southernct.edu/Chinese-Americans.

[2] Mary Hanna and Jeanne Batalova, "Immigrants from Asia in the United States," Migration Policy Institute, March 10 2021, www.migrationpolicy.org/article/immigrants-asia-united-states-2020.

Unbecoming

itself. During the Gold Rush of 1849, many Chinese immigrants who dreamt of riches settled on the West Coast. By the end of the 1850s, Chinese immigrants made up one-fifth of the population that constituted the Southern Mines.[3] At first, the Chinese workers were praised for their cleanliness and hardworking nature. However, as the gold supply thinned, white workers accused Chinese workers of stealing their wealth.

One of the manifestations of this racial tension was the Chinese Massacre of 1871, in which eighteen Chinese men were lynched and killed by a mob of over five hundred in Los Angeles.[4] Violence and assaults toward the Chinese were not uncommon during this era, as many more incidents occurred all over the West Coast and Midwest. In Rock Springs, Wyoming, and Tacoma, Washington, Chinese people were killed, brutalized, and driven out of their homes.[5]

At the same time, media portrayals of Asian Americans invoked Yellow Peril imagery. These illustrations emphasized and caricatured the "exotic" features and skin color of Asian Americans. They depicted East Asians with slanted eyes, devilish features, yellowed skin, long queues, and generally

---

[3] "Chinese Immigrants and the Gold Rush," Public Broadcasting Service, accessed on May 21, 2021, www.pbs.org/wgbh/americanexperience/features/goldrush-chinese-immigrants/.

[4] Kelly Wallace, "Forgotten Los Angeles History: The Chinese Massacre of 1871," Los Angeles Public Library, May 19, 2017, www.lapl.org/collections-resources/blogs/lapl/chinese-massacre-1871.

[5] History.com Editors. "The Rock Springs Massacre," History.com, April 13, 2021, www.history.com/topics/immigration/rock-springs-massacre-wyoming.

ugly expressions.[6] The messaging of this easily-disseminated media was not hard to miss: Asian immigrants were evil outsiders who corrupted Western ideals and were to blame for the lack of economic opportunities.

In 1882, at the height of anti-Chinese sentiment, the Chinese Exclusion Act was passed, which prohibited the immigration of all Chinese laborers. After its passage, the U.S. had an active agenda in further barring Asians from entry into the country. The Immigration Act of 1924 established a national origins quota system, systematically excluding other undesirable ethnic groups such as Hindus, Indians, Japanese, and more.[7]

The discrimination that the Asian American community faces today is just as harmful as that of the late 19th and 20th centuries. During the COVID-19 pandemic, Asian Americans are still being pushed, slashed, verbally assaulted, and murdered for something that they did not cause. From March 19, 2020, to February 28, 2021, the nonprofit organization Stop Asian American Hate recorded a total of 3,795 racial hate incidents towards Asian Americans.[8] This is most likely only a small portion of the total number of hate crimes and incidents because many go unreported out of fear.[9]

---

[6] "Asian Immigration: The 'Yellow Peril,'" BGSU University Libraries, accessed on May 21, 2021, digitalgallery.bgsu.edu/student/exhibits/show/race-in-us/asian-americans/asian-immigration-and-the--yel.

[7] History.com Staff, "Chinese Exclusion Act," History.com, August 24, 2018, www.history.com/topics/immigration/chinese-exclusion-act-1882.

[8] Russell Jeung et al., "STOP AAPI HATE NATIONAL REPORT," Stop AAPI Hate, accessed on May 21, 2021, https://stopaapihate.org/2020-2021-national-report/.

[9] Catherine Thorbecke, "Why Anti-Asian Hate Incidents Often Go Unreported and How to Help," ABC News, March 18, 2021,

Although many of us were born in America or have lived in America for most of our lives, we are placed under the perpetual foreigner stereotype. We are told, "Go back to your country," or are persistently nagged with the question, "But where are you *really* from?" No matter how much Asian Americans, both past and present, have contributed to the United States, it is assumed that we will never be able to assimilate; we will always be a frightening, foreign minority—the Yellow Peril.

There is a clear pattern in how U.S. history is being taught in our classrooms. Although I have learned—and relearned, year after year—about George Washington, Christopher Columbus, Thomas Jefferson, and Martin Luther King, Jr., I never learned about Asian American historical figures. Very rarely are Asian Americans discussed in U.S. history in ways that are separate from their labor and economic contributions; I learned about Chinese miners during the Gold Rush but not about activists like Yuri Kochiyama, who participated in cross-racial solidarity and Black-Asian political movements.

The centuries-long history of anti-Asian racism is why it is crucial that we adjust New York State's social studies curricula to include more Asian American visibility in U.S. history classes. Protests and donations to Asian American organizations may help to condemn and raise awareness of anti-Asian racism, but there is another solution. To address both the long history and recent surges of anti-Asian bias, which are founded in ignorance and lack of active anti-racist teaching, we must start at the root of the problem: education.

---

abcnews.go.com/US/anti-asian-hate-incidents-unreported/story?id=76509072.

Bias is not inherited but learned. Children are not born with the belief that others are inferior because of their race or some other characteristic. They learn to discriminate against others because of their environment. But in early childhood, education has a large impact on a child's worldview, and we could counteract some of the damage done by parents and the media by incorporating Asian American stories, historical figures, and struggles into school curricula. We can begin the very important work of active antiracist teaching in our classrooms. Only after Asian Americans are highlighted in school curricula can we most accurately and responsibly convey the rich history of the United States.

Some schools may hesitate to incorporate such information because they don't want to "talk about race" in the classroom. Yet as the primary vessel bestowing knowledge to young impressionable minds, schools should be the first place where the concept of racism is acknowledged and introduced to students in a controlled manner. Engaging in antiracist education should be key for schools; when the history of racism against Asian Americans is not acknowledged, it decontextualizes the recent surges in anti-Asian hate during the COVID-19 pandemic. How can the New York State Education Department stay silent through nonaction when both our past and present are revealing this pattern of hate towards Asian Americans so clearly?

What is included in the Curricula

One evident error with the New York State history curriculum is that it focuses on only a few milestones in Asian American history: the Gold Rush, Asian laborers, helping to build the Transcontinental Railroad, the Chinese Exclusion Act of 1882, and the incarceration of Japanese Americans during World War II. However, these historical fragments fail to fully represent Asian American history. In reality, Asians have impacted every single part of our economy and collective American culture since the first wave of Asian immigration in the late 19th century. And yet, Asian Americans in American politics, pop culture, and activism are covered only in a short paragraph in our textbook sections, if at all.

The discrimination against Asian Americans described in New York State history textbooks is almost exclusively related to their labor contributions or the alleged robbery of economic opportunity that they committed against white laborers. In contrast, contributions to politics and popular culture are rarely or never mentioned. More often than not, Asian Americans are portrayed only as laborers and nothing else. This is implicit messaging that Asian immigrants to the U.S. are inseparable from their labor, devoid of civic engagement and politicalness.

Asian Americans' individuality is often stripped as they are confined to a single stereotype: quiet, obedient workers who don't quite count as people of color in America's Black and white binary—the model minority. However, this image of Asian Americans is often limited to East Asians, while South and Southeast Asians are neglected. Many South Asian Americans have expressed that they are excluded from the Asian American community because of cultural or religious differences.[10] They

---

[10] Kevin Nadal, "The Brown Asian American Movement: Advocating for South Asian, Southeast Asian, and Filipino American Communities," Harvard Kennedy School Student Publication, February 2, 2020, aapr.hkspublications.org/2020/02/02/the-

are severely underrepresented in media and Asian American Studies. The Asian American milestones currently covered in the New York State history curriculum only discuss the experiences of Chinese or Japanese Americans. As a result, many students' impressions of Asians are that they are only of Chinese, Japanese, or Korean heritage. In other words, the history curriculum now perpetuates the perception that Asian Americans are light-skinned; the curriculum fails to recognize dark-skinned Asians from countries such as India, Laos, Bangladesh, the Philippines, and Cambodia, to name a few.

What should be included in the Curricula

Asian American history is not composed of only tragedies and discrimination. While these events are essential areas that should be taught, our history is also rich in cultural and political contributions. Court cases involving Asian Americans are important to include in the New York State U.S. history curriculum because they directly challenge the model minority stereotype that generalizes all Asian Americans as polite, law-abiding, and silent even when they are suffering. These struggles in the legal system convey a different story: that Asian Americans, since their very first mass migration to the United States, have been agitating at the highest judicial level, the Supreme Court, for their civil rights. The current New York State U.S. history curriculum includes the court case *Korematsu* v. *United States*, but there were plenty of other cases spurred by Asian Americans challenging unjust laws and policies. Many civil

---

brown-asian-american-movement-advocating-for-south-asian-southeast-asian-and-filipino-american-communities/.

liberties and services that many students may enjoy today, such as birthright citizenship and supplementary English classes, can be traced back to the brave Asian Americans who challenged inequitable laws on the highest level of the judicial system.

One notable example is *United States v. Wong Kim Ark*, which was decided on March 28, 1898. Wong Kim Ark was born in San Francisco, yet was denied re-entry after he traveled from China for a family visit because of the Chinese Exclusion Act. The Supreme Court ruled in favor of Ark, and this case led to the establishment of the concept of jus soli, which states that children born in the United States are citizens even if their parents are not.[11] Students would benefit greatly from studying the *United States v. Wong Kim Ark* case because the concepts of jus soli and birthright citizenship are still relevant today, entering contemporary discourse about immigration.

Similarly, nine-year-old Martha Lum was denied entry into an educational institution because of her race. Though she was born in the United States and her parents were tax-paying citizens, she was not allowed to attend the all-white Rosedale Consolidated School because "she was of Chinese descent, and not a member of the white or Caucasian race."[12] As a result, Martha's father filed a lawsuit. In 1927, the Supreme Court ruled 9-0 in *Gong Lum v. Rice* that the Mississippi school board did not violate the Fourteenth Amendment's equal protection

---

[11] "United States v. Wong Kim Ark," Oyez, accessed May 21, 2021, https://www.oyez.org/cases/1850-1900/169us649.

[12] Mark Gooden, "Gong Lum v. Rice," Encyclopædia Britannica, September 5, 2014, https://www.britannica.com/event/Gong-Lum-v-Rice.

clause when denying Martha's enrollment.[13] Although the Lum family did not win the court case, this event is still significant because it challenges a deep-rooted belief from that time period that minority groups simply accepted their unfair treatment. *Gong Lum v. Rice* laid the path for many more Asian Americans to speak out against injustice. From this example, students will learn the importance of addressing bias in historical events where the Asian American minority was oppressed.

The court case *Lau v. Nichols* further demonstrates persistent efforts by Asian Americans for equal opportunities. In 1971, the San Francisco school system was established, absorbing over 2,500 students of Chinese descent who were not fluent in English. Despite this, the school system taught classes exclusively in English and only provided supplemental English courses to about 1,000 students.[14] Kinney Kinmon Lau and other Chinese American students brought a class action suit against the officials in the San Francisco Unified School District, claiming that this failure to present equal educational opportunities to every student violated the Fourteenth Amendment and the Civil Rights Act of 1964. The Supreme Court ruled that the San Francisco Unified School District indeed violated the Civil Rights Act, resulting in Chinese students receiving unfair public school education.[15] This ruling was especially important, as it pushed public schools to develop supplemental language instruction and eased the transition into education

---

[13] Gooden, "Gong Lum v. Rice."
[14] "Lau v. Nichols," Oyez, accessed May 21, 2021, www.oyez.org/cases/1973/72-6520.
[15] Susan Bon, "Lau v. Nichols," Encyclopædia Britannica, September 9, 2014, www.britannica.com/topic/Lau-v-Nichols.

for students who did not speak English. Incorporating this court case into the New York State U.S. history curriculum may create a moment of reflection for students, prompting them to consider whether their schools adequately support immigrant and non-English-speaking students.

These court cases revolved around discriminatory laws against Asian Americans. The brave Asian Americans involved exposed their personal information and risked public lash back in order to push for racial equality and protection under the law. Though they were not always successful, the actions that they took in the legal system again demonstrate the untruths in the model minority stereotype that is so readily ascribed to Asian Americans.

In particular, hate targeted towards Southeast Asians is not acknowledged in both students' daily lives and in their classes. After the September 11 attacks, many Southeast Asians, especially Muslims, or those who appeared to be Muslim, were targeted. Across the U.S., individuals with white supremacist ideologies carried out attacks against individuals that they racially profiled to be Arab American. One even went as far as murder. Balbir Singh Sodhi, a Sikh American with no ties to al-Qaeda, was murdered on September 15, 2001. He was shot in the Arizona gas station that he owned by Frank Roque, who wanted to "kill a Muslim" in retaliation for the 9/11 attacks. Sodhi was the first reported hate crime victim post-9/11, but he was not the last.

The tragic events of 9/11 induced fear, hatred, and panic in many Americans. When people are subjected to unknowns and crises, they often place the blame on certain minorities who cannot fight back. The parallels between the post-9/11 hate crimes against South Asians are disturbingly similar to those against Asian Americans during the COVID-19 pandemic, as well as those against Chinese Americans following the Gold Rush. These instances of violence and racial scapegoating are crucial events that need to be covered in the New York State U.S. history curriculum in order to teach students how to think rationally and in a way that is anti-prejudice when crises and tragedies occur. Unfortunately, the same kind of bias and racism that led to the massacres of Chinese miners in the late 19th century and the murders of countless South Asians following 9/11 is still persistent now; the New York State Education Department has a responsibility to draw the connections between the past and the present for the advancement of Asian Americans.

Additionally, one significant yet often overlooked aspect of Asian American history is the ways in which it intersects and overlaps with the histories of other marginalized peoples.

After the Emancipation Proclamation, Asian laborers, or "coolies," were, for some time, considered to be a viable alternative to slave labor in the American South. These Chinese laborers were described as "entirely inhuman" and "the ideal industrial machine which needed less food and less remuneration for more work in less time."[16] Chinese coolies were seen as human technologies that were even better than emancipated slaves because they were more obedient, and they were considered better than white workers because they were more

---

[16] Matthew Pratt Guterl, "After Slavery: Asian Labor, the American South, and the Age of Emancipation," *Journal of World History*, vol. 14, no. 2, (2003): 209-241, www.jstor.org/stable/20079206.

efficient.[17] Workers were constantly abused and whipped by the overseers, with many coolies committing suicide in order to escape this cruel fate.[18] The exploitation of Chinese coolies in the American South is an aspect of the post-Civil War era that is rarely taught. The experiences of Chinese laborers in the post-Emancipation American South should be included in the New York State U.S. history curriculum because it adds nuance to the discussion of the Black and white racial binary in the U.S. during and after the Civil War.

Another interesting topic to consider is the ways in which South Asians occupied a middle position in the segregated South's racial hierarchy. Segregation and Jim Crow, as are currently taught in history classes, are limited to a Black and white binary. What remains to be explored, however, is the position of South Asians in that racial hierarchy. Although some courts and documents classified Indians as "white," most were still segregated to live in African American communities.[19] Many South Asian men married Black women. A prime example of bringing up is Moksad Ali, an Indian man who married an African American woman named Ella Blackman. Ali was allowed to move within Southern society more freely than his wife was, despite his skin being darker than Blackman's.[20] Introducing the long history of South Asians in the American South is a crucial avenue through which to explore how segregation and the Black-white racial binary

---

[17] Guterl, "After Slavery," 209-241.

[18] Guterl, "After Slavery," 209-241.

[19] "Early South Asian Immigration," Asian Americans Advancing Justice, accessed on May 21, 2021, https://advancingjustice-la.org/what-we-do/curriculum-lesson-plans/asian-americans-k-12-education-curriculum/episode-1-lesson-6.

[20] "Early South Asian Immigration."

impacted Asian Americans. South Asians were considered white on paper and enjoyed benefits that were denied to their Black counterparts, yet were still subject to segregation and discrimination. Investigating this topic would offer a historical perspective on a contradiction that many Asian Americans today still experience: being perceived as the white-adjacent model minority, yet still the victim of intolerance and racial animus.

In Asian American activism, there has also been a long history of cross-racial solidarity and Black-Asian political movements. Yuri Kochiyama, for example, was a Japanese American political activist who dedicated her life to social change through her participation in social justice movements, which were often cross-racial and intersectional. Her father had been arrested and detained by the FBI after the bombing of Pearl Harbor because agents suspected, without evidence, that he had ties to the Japanese emperor. His death after being severely weakened by the detainment prompted Kochiyama to pursue a future in political activism.[21] In the 1960s, Kochiyama participated in the Asian American, Black, and Third World Liberation movements to fight for civil rights and an ethics studies program at universities. She also protested the war in Vietnam, which she saw as racist and imperialist.[22] She worked closely with the Black activist Malcolm X, fighting for racial justice and human rights, and was active in the reparations movement for Japanese Americans. She spoke out

---

[21] "May 19, 1921: Yuri Kochiyama Born," Zinn Education Project, accessed on May 21, 2021,
https://www.zinnedproject.org/news/tdih/yuri-kochiyama-was-born/.

[22] "Yuri Kochiyama Born."

for communities of all colors and was a strong Asian American political figure. For her contributions to the Civil Rights Movement and her strong advocacy for Japanese American rights, Kochiyama should be covered in the New York State U.S. history curriculum. Kochiyama's life and work in agitating for the civil rights of all Americans reveal the close collaboration between Asian Americans and Black Americans, which is often neglected in history classes.

Another Asian American figure who worked cross-racially was Larry Itliong, a Filipino American labor organizer who had a pivotal role in the farm labor movement. During his political career, he organized many strikes and boycotts. In 1965, he led the Delano grape strike and contacted the Chicano American labor activist Cesar Chavez to join the strike. [23] A year later, the Agricultural Workers Organizing Committee, mainly composed of Filipino American laborers, and the National Farm Workers Association, made up of mostly Chicano American laborers, joined together to create the United Farm Workers (UFW), a labor union that forever changed the face of agricultural labor in California. [24] The formation of the UFW represented the close collaboration of Asian and Latinx migrant farmworkers in the simultaneous struggles against racism and capitalism. Yet while recognition grew for Chavez, Itliong's contributions were scarcely mentioned. Although the Delano grape strike was

---

[23] Gayle Romasanta, "Why It Is Important to Know the Story of Filipino-American Larry Itliong," *Smithsonian Magazine*, July 24, 2019, https://www.smithsonianmag.com/smithsonian-institution/why-it-is-important-know-story-filipino-american-larry-itliong-180972696/.

[24] Romasanta, "Larry Itliong."

one of the most significant labor movements in American history, many people, including many Filipino Americans themselves, are unaware of Itliong's pivotal role in organizing the workers. Including Itliong in the New York State U.S. history curriculum would expose students to not only the experiences of Filipino Americans but the experiences of migrant Filipino farm workers as well.

The fight for equal rights has been constant throughout American history, and it is often one that engages many different groups and social identities. By 1968, many Asian American activists were inspired by the organization and work of the Black Power movement. In that year, the Asian American Political Alliance (AAPA) was formed, bringing together disparate ethnic groups of Asian students for the first time. Asian American student activists advocated for more faculty and students of color, as well as the end of the Vietnam War, police brutality, and the exploitation of migrant Asian farm workers.[25] It was clear that this generation of Asian Americans wanted to break their stereotype as meek and apologetic foreigners. The AAPA was very active in the political discussion of the era; the organization screened films and sponsored panels on socialism, the Chinese Revolution, class struggle, and anti-war activities.

Again, Asian American history here is intertwined with the histories of other marginalized, oppressed peoples in the U.S. Early on in the Yellow Power movement, Asian Americans recognized how much

---

[25] Jeffery Ogbar, "Yellow Power: The Formation of Asian American Nationalism in the Age of Black Power, 1966-1975," *Souls Journal*, vol. 3, no. 3 (2001): 29-37, https://doi.org/10.1080/10999949.2001.12098172.

of their own political education and mobilization was influenced by the Black Power movement, and how much-marginalized peoples could benefit from cross-racial and cross-ethnic solidarity. Declaring alliance with Chicano and Black Americans, the AAPA stated, "We Asian-Americans support all non-white liberation movements."[26] Coalitions with non-Asian American groups were formed, and the Yellow Power Movement agitated for common goals. For example, Asian Americans were heavily involved with the Third World Liberation Front (TWLF), a cross-racial, cross-ethnic student alliance among Black Americans, Asian Americans, Chicano Americans, and Indigenous Americans, among others. Together, these student groups brought campus reforms and demanded an ethnic studies program at San Francisco State University in what came to be the longest student strike in U.S. history.[27] The TWLF's goals are still relevant today, and learning about this inclusive coalition will enable students to see the importance of activism and the connections between the TWLF's demands and contemporary demands to make school curricula more representative. Through a more culturally diverse curriculum, students will be able to learn about their community's history and develop an antiracist mindset.

 The success of the Third World Liberation Front relied on the unity of many marginalized groups in the U.S. Including this history of cross-racial and cross-ethnic solidarity in the New York State history curriculum is crucial; students will learn the

---

[26] Ogbar, "Yellow Power," 29-37.
[27] "The Third World Liberation Front," The Berkeley Revolution, accessed on May 21, 2021,
http://revolution.berkeley.edu/projects/twlf/.

historical causes and effects of cross-racial solidarity in the fight for liberation. This takeaway can easily be connected to modern-day discourse about the necessity of cross-racial and cross-ethnic alliances in activism.

Conclusion

As the nation faces a rise of anti-Asian sentiment, we need to educate our students about Asian American history. Although Asian Americans have played a large role in the political and economic establishments of the United States, they are frequently viewed as perpetual foreigners who will never truly assimilate.

Mere fragments of Asian American accomplishments and sufferings are taught, failing to capture the richness of our history. Political figures, court cases, intimacies between Asian Americans and other marginalized peoples, Asian Americans in activism, and South Asian American history are all missing from the curriculum. They should be included. Because Asian American history is present in every aspect of American history, teachers would only need to add Asian American figures and perspectives to events that are already outlined in the curriculum.

In addition to modifying the curriculum, hiring and recruiting more Asian American educators may rectify the lack of Asian American visibility in U.S. history classes. Within the teaching profession, Asian Americans only comprise two percent of educators. Children of different ethnicities often find comfort in learning from someone of a similar culture, appearance, or language as them. The absence of non-Asian teachers deprives Asian American students of a role model in their early childhoods.[28] Additionally, more Asian American teachers in the classroom will provide more positive representations of Asian Americans. Teachers often supplement the standard curriculum with their own anecdotes and mini-lessons, and they often choose particular areas to highlight because of personal connection or interest. Diversifying the teaching workforce will enable Asian Americans to be heard in educational decisions and create a comfortable atmosphere for Asian Americans students.

Although I hope that future textbook editions will include more diverse Asian American history, it will take years or decades for these textbooks to be updated. Therefore, the information that I have covered in this essay will likely not be included in school textbooks soon. Teachers should consider resources and activities outside of the textbook in order to educate students about Asian American history. Examples include class discussions, individual and group research projects, and more.

Many Asian American and antiracist organizations have already compiled curricula that can be adapted into the existing New York State U.S. history curricula. Because these resources exist, adding more activities, discussions, and lessons throughout the year in which students can learn about Asian American history should not be very time-consuming or costly for school boards and teachers.

The State of Connecticut has already introduced HB-6619, an act to "develop a model curriculum for grades kindergarten to grade eight, inclusive, for use

---

[28] George Huynh, "Recruiting and Retaining Asian American Teachers," Education Studies, accessed on May 21, 2021, http://debsedstudies.org/asian-american-teachers/.

by local and regional boards of education."[29] This act requires schools to integrate topics such as Native American studies, Asian Pacific American studies,

---

[29] "Substitute for Raised H.B. No. 6619 Session Year 2021," Connecticut General Assembly, March 11, 2021, www.cga.ct.gov/asp/cgabillstatus/cgabillstatus.asp?selBillType=Bill&bill_num=HB06619&which_year=2021.

Chapter 4

Challenging Myself

(eleventh grade - now)

Potstickers

NCTE Superior Writing Certificate Winner, Published on LICAA

"Ugh, I think she's eating a dog!" a spiked-hair boy next to me wailed to his friends.

I sat in my middle school cafeteria, frozen in fear. I had brought potstickers for lunch for the first time. Although the PB&J at my school was delicious, I was craving something comforting and familiar. Yet when I opened my lunch bag to enjoy my meal, this startling outcry drew everyone's attention to the opened container I had in front of me.

Someone next to me groaned about the strange smell coming from the container. Another girl shouted from her table that it smelled like three-day-old fish. And it got worse. Others walked by, clutching grilled cheese sandwiches and making obnoxious gagging noises. Instead of yelling back or reporting them to the teacher, I sat there silently and pretended that their laughter didn't bother me, suppressing my tears.

"Don't cry, Iris," a small boy said. "We're only joking."

Yes, it was only a joke, but to 11-year-old Iris, those comments shattered my world. Before that moment, I had never been ashamed of my culture. It was the most precious part of my identity, where I could find treasured memories of making dumplings with my family or receiving red packets to buy snacks on New Year's. But sitting in that cafeteria made me wish I could run away and throw away the potstickers that I used to enjoy so much.

Now more than ever, Asian Americans are being verbally and physically harassed and blamed for problems that we cannot control. Although many of us were born in America or have lived in America for most of our lives, we are treated like unwelcome foreigners. We are told, "Go back to your country," or are persistently nagged with the question, "But where are you really from?" We are boiled down to being the "Virus," derogatory slurs, weirdly misshapen eyes, and misconstrued cultural traditions. We are being kicked down in broad daylight, slashed, burned, killed, and assaulted. No matter how much Asian Americans have contributed to the United States, it is assumed that we will never be able to assimilate; we will always be a frightening, foreign minority—the Yellow Peril.

While progressive movements and protests have brought advancements in the struggle for equality in the United States, the increase of hate and violence towards Asian Americans over the past two years and the history of scapegoating Asian immigrants for economic or social issues have made it clear that the problem of racial discrimination is far from over.

At the same time, we can't be optimistic without being aware of what's happening in the world. Naive optimism that avoids addressing the problems that plague our society today is a form of ignorance.

Instead, we should possess a nuanced optimism in which we are aware of the urgency and consequences of these social issues and do everything in our power to bring change to them–truly believing that change can occur. And to begin addressing this bias founded in ignorance and introducing anti-racist ideas to our children, we must start at the root of the problem: education. There is a clear pattern in how U.S. history is being taught in our classrooms. Although I have learned—and relearned, year after year—about George Washington, Christopher Columbus, Thomas Jefferson, and Martin Luther King, Jr., I have never learned the history of Asian Americans in any of my classes. Not to mention the fact that the curriculum severely underrepresents South Asians from countries such as India, Laos, Bangladesh, the Philippines, and Cambodia, to name a few.

Very rarely are Asian Americans discussed in U.S. history in ways that are separate from their labor and economic contributions. While these events are important, our history is also rich in cultural and political contributions. For example, Asian American activists have exposed their personal information and risked public backlash in order to advocate for racial equality and protection. Their actions demonstrate the model minority stereotype, the stigma that all Asian Americans are docile and politically passive, is untrue.

Bias is not inherited but learned. Children are not born with the belief that others are inferior because of their race or some other characteristic. They learn to discriminate against others because of their environment. But in early childhood, education has a large impact on a child's worldview, and we could counteract some of the damage done by environments and the media by incorporating Asian American stories, historical figures, and struggles into school curricula. We can begin the very important work of active antiracist teaching in our classrooms. Only after Asian Americans are highlighted in school curricula can we most accurately and responsibly convey the rich history of the United States.

What a single 16-year-old girl can do in the face of racism, a problem that has plagued the country since its founding, may seem inconsequential; but the voices of thousands of people within a community that has suffered the same discrimination can make a difference. Each time I speak my mind about the bias my community faces, each time I sign a petition, each time I refuse to have my justice denied, is yet another step toward a hopeful future in which an Asian girl will no longer have to suffer through mockery towards her culture and will be able to enjoy her potstickers at the cafeteria table.

The Quiet Girl

Speech delivered at the Great Neck AAPI Bill Rally

Thank you, everyone. And thank you for giving me the opportunity to speak at this rally. It is a pleasure and an honor to be here today.

In school, I'm "the quiet girl." I've always been "the quiet girl." During recess, I, like many other "quiet girls," preferred to read a book in the comforts of my school's library instead of playing tag with the students outside. Rather than chatting with the teacher about the latest NBA game before class, I draw in my notebook. I have always been the listener, never the speaker. Until recently, I had never been the one to take action.

As "the quiet girl," I know that being quiet comes with its consequences. People will make assumptions about you, ignore you, disregard your opinion, and waive your rights. I refuse to continue to be the "quiet girl." And the Asian American community, as we face the continued violation of our fundamental rights, cannot remain quiet in the corner of the classroom. Because if we do, American society will forever remain unchanged.

Two years ago, COVID shut down our world, and almost overnight, the Asian American community was met with more hate crimes than we have ever seen.

Why should we be afraid to walk in our own community? Why should we hesitate to go to the supermarket in fear of crazed attacks, harassment, slashings, pushings, and hospitalization? This is our home too. And it is time we tackle this bigoted bias against our community in a place where our contributions to society and our voices have been ignored: in our classrooms.

Education prepares students for their integration into a diverse and complex society. But how can we be prepared to enter this world if we are not given a full view of American history? We need to incorporate Asian American historical figures, struggles, and stories into the school curriculum. Only then can we begin the very important work of erasing anti-Asian bias and ensuring that the tragedies of yesterday and today do not occur tomorrow.

If this bill is passed, then American citizens and politicians will learn that we are not perpetual foreigners. We are not the "Yellow Peril" that plagues the streets of their beloved cities and towns. We are not a threat. We are the fabric of America. We are political activists. We are doctors. We are chefs, teachers, judges, factory workers, lawyers, mothers and fathers, and students. We are a community that has the right to walk these streets unafraid of being harmed or murdered. We can no longer be ignored as an integral part of American history and American society. We are hurt, we are bleeding, and our voices are demanding to be heard. So let them hear us. With this, I resolve to no longer be the quiet girl. Thank you.

We Are Not Victims - Why the Asian and Black Community needs Coalition

Delivered at Asian and Black Coalition rally on 8/5

Thank you to KACE and everyone here tonight for giving me this valuable opportunity to share my thoughts at this rally.

Starting from 2020, "Stick together. Don't get hate crimed." became a casual passerby joke for my friends and me. We say it with humor because doing so makes the grim reality that any of us could be pushed down to the boardwalk and assaulted just for our ethnicity easier to deal with. But the context behind this joke is nothing to laugh at.

But I've also since noticed a strange pattern. Whenever we have conversations about racial prejudice, we have to bring one marginalized community down in order to bring another one up. Then the conversation will eventually escalate into a heated debate about which community is treated worse - rather than coming to a collaborative solution of why we should all be treated better.

A quick scan of a Wechat group, a youtube comment section, or a Facebook message board shows the reality of the tension between a lot of people in the Asian and black communities. Prejudice, stereotypes, and heated online debates. Whatever it is, it all seems to communicate one message: Black people and Asian people don't get along.

But, other instances from history and recent days tell a different tale. In the 1960s, when Fred Hampton, chairman of the Black Panther Party, stood in front of a multiracial group and shouted

"Black Power to Black People. Yellow Power to Yellow People. Or that of Yuri Kochiyama, a Japanese immigrant woman who advocated for both Asian and black rights, who decades later held the body of Malcolm X after his assassination. From the present movements of Asians for black lives to black power for anti-Asian violence.

We need a Black and Asian coalition because both of our marginalized communities share the same problem: bias of education.

Right now, the Asian American history we see in our textbooks is limited to this singular narrative: Asian Americans are victims. We are victims of the Chinese Exclusion Act. We are victims of Japanese internment camps. We are victims of lynching and prosecution, and racial prejudice. We are victims and nothing more.

If it wasn't for the research I did in advance in order to speak knowledgeably about both Black and Asian history today, the only black history I would know is Martin Luther King, Malcolm X, Rosa Parks, and slavery.

(PAUSE)

But that is not who we are.

There is more to both of our communities than just pain and suffering.

Our communities are full of change-makers and leaders. Our communities are vibrant. They're made up of people risking their livelihood to better this society, and they're made up of people making an effort to communicate and work with other struggling marginalized communities despite their differences. But right now. Most of us, especially students who will become future participants in American society, have learned nothing about these communities.

But we have an opportunity today. With the passage of the Senate Bill (S6359A), AAPI stories about loss, struggles, change, and hope will be added as a standard part of our arsenal in our war against ignorance and our journey to understanding. These stories of solidarity will inspire conversations happening NOW about how we can come to collaborative solutions together.

My name is Iris Liu, I am a rising senior that attends Manhasset High School, and I'm the president of Acknowledge Our History. (pause, tone change as if telling a secret) And I have a confession to make: There's only one black kid in my grade, and I don't know many black people. I would confidently guess that many Asian people in the audience share my situation. But we can do something to change that, so let's start today.

What Does Being An Immigrant Mean?

My heart was soaring. I couldn't believe an actual reporter wanted to interview me! My face flushed as I talked about the articles I'd published about the 2020 election.

Suddenly, the reporter interrupted me. "Iris, if you wouldn't mind me asking. You said that you immigrated to America. Do you have a green card?"

"I do."

"Oh, I see."

After a few pleasantries, the reporter quickly hung up. I was confused; I wasn't done talking.

The reporter later called and informed my mom that they were only looking to interview American citizens and that I was merely a permanent resident. I felt helpless and stunned. Despite the controversies around immigration status and "illegal" immigrants, I had never imagined that all the value of my hard work and writing could be erased because of a plastic card. I have legal proof that I should be here after all; doesn't that make me more of an "American" than the "illegal" immigrants?

When I first heard the debate over "illegal" immigrants and building a wall, I thought that if Americans wanted to spend that much money to keep someone out of the country, they must be terrible people. All I have ever read about *illegal immigrants* were numbers, quotes from politicians, and various amounts of text about how these *uneducated illegals* brought crime into the country. What reason did I have to think otherwise?

But being rejected by the reporter compelled me to learn more about what immigration means. Who are these *illegals*? Who would willingly leave their home and their family to pursue a country where they cannot legally work, vote, or benefit from social services? Many *illegals* are treated like pests that need to be exterminated.

Undocumented immigrants do not bring crime into this country. They have substantially lower crime rates than native-born citizens and legal immigrants. US-born citizens are over twice as likely to be arrested for violent crimes than undocumented immigrants. In the USA, at least 250,000 undocumented college students pursue higher education to better their lives. They can be journalists, students, chefs, caretakers, and activists who dedicate their lives to making a change--a reality far from the one-faceted image of a poorly educated and violent community that the media often portrays.

To correct this biased image, we need to tell their stories. The newspapers should provide a platform for undocumented immigrants to speak out on their struggles. TV news should feature reports on undocumented immigrants' journey and life in America. By telling their stories, we can learn about the mother of three who loves her children and moved to this country to provide a better life, or the high school student with all A's in STEM but no college to attend, or the kid who grew up in America, but was told that he would never assimilate.

My privilege has allowed me to live an ignorant life, unaware and uncaring of the struggles of these undocumented immigrants. I didn't face possible deportation as I went about my daily life. Nor did I suffer the frustrations of being unable to work or get financial aid. The others don't have this opportunity, and we must eradicate the unceasing framing of these undocumented immigrants as an uneducated, violent, and faceless mass. They are human beings struggling to get by -- a story that every one of us should be able to relate to.

Many Thanks to the Following:

Long Island Chinese American Association - for funding the publication of 'Unbecoming'

Manhasset Association of Chinese Americans - for being the best and most accepting community I could ever ask for. The passionate individuals in this organization always have intricately planned events to promote Asian American culture in our community.

Assemblywoman Gina Sillitti, Christine Liu, Janet Lavin, and Mario Ferone - for giving me the opportunity for participating in local activism and politics.
Our discussions about local events and the political process are always informative and engaging.

Guodong Zhang - for supporting many of my writing endeavors. You were the one who introduced me to AAPI Activism and I cannot thank you enough for that. Thank you for giving my writing a platform and for all the work you've done for the Chinese American community.

Jonathan Kravetz - for helping me pursue my passion for creative writing. Talking with you can always push me to advance my writing techniques and ideas. I don't think I will ever forget the process of writing Dream Baker.

Richard In - for his consideration and guidance in many of my projects. You always have really interesting points about AAPI History and project timelines.
Your eiciency and activism are inspiring.

Youngsoo Choi - for reaching out to me and allowing me to share my writing with the Korean American community. I am so happy that my writing was able to reach more people. Thank you.

Eileen Madigan-Behrmann - for introducing me to different writing genres, jumpstarting my interest in speech writing, and giving me engaging insights into my writing. You are my favorite English Teacher.

Kristen Ruthkowski - for listening to me talk about my projects and giving me the much-needed help throughout these high school years. Thank you for being the best counselor a student could ask for.

Dilshad Dayani - for teaching me about the stories about Undocumented immigrants and reinvigorating my interest in Op-Ed writing. The discussions in your class were genuinely eye-opening.

And **my family**, for their patience and love.

CPSIA information can be obtained
at www.ICGtesting.com
Printed in the USA
BVHW031146031022
648542BV00014B/463